Georgia's Girlhood Embroidery:
"Crowned with Glory and Immortality"

Kathleen Staples

National Endowment for the Arts
arts.gov

Printed in China in an edition of 1,000 by Kings Time Printing Press, Ltd.

Design: The Adsmith
Department of Publications: Hillary Brown and Stella Tran
Publications Interns: Gais Chowdhury and Rebecca Stapleford

Names: Staples, Kathleen A., author. | Georgia Museum of Art, organizer, host institution.
Title: Georgia's girlhood embroidery : "crowned with glory and immortality" / Kathleen Staples.
Description: Athens, GA : Georgia Museum of Art, University of Georgia, 201. | "October 31, 2015/February 28, 2016." | Includes bibliographical references.
Identifiers: LCCN 2015040175| ISBN 9780915977918 (alk. paper) | ISBN 0915977915
Subjects: LCSH: Samplers--Georgia--History--18th century--Exhibitions. | Samplers--Georgia--History--19th century--Exhibitions.
Classification: LCC NK9112 .S725 2015 | DDC 746.44--dc23
LC record available at http://lccn.loc.gov/2015040175

This project is supported in part by a grant from the National Endowment for the Arts. To find out more about how NEA grants impact individuals and communities, visit www.arts.gov. Robert and Suzanne Currey and Howard and Helen Elkins also provided financial support, as did the W. Newton Morris Charitable Foundation and the Friends of the Georgia Museum of Art.

Georgia's Girlhood Embroidery: "Crowned with Glory and Immortality"

Kathleen Staples

with essays by **Dale L. Couch** and **Jenny Garwood**

Georgia Museum of Art
Athens, Georgia

October 31, 2015–February 28, 2016

A human being given up to ignorance, and self will, is infinitely below the most abject brute: the same creature trained by virtuous exertions to the highest perfection Literature affords, to be little lower than the Angels, and will be crowned with glory and Immortality!

—excerpt from newspaper advertisement for ladies' academy, "Mount of Health," *Augusta Chronicle*, December 11, 1812

TABLE OF CONTENTS

FOREWORD

One of the great joys of studying objects is how often that study leads to a winding journey through the byways of history, culminating in an unexpected discovery that illuminates some aspect of the past like a searchlight. When a researcher starts with a piece of needlework, it prompts a series of questions about the life of its maker, the nature of its materials, and the culture that influenced its creation. Today, most of us are far removed from the basics of how the textiles we use in our daily lives are produced. In preindustrial times, and even well into the nineteenth century, this was not the case. Cloth—and clothing—took far more time to make and consumed a far larger proportion of a family's available income than it does today. The international trade in textiles linked the United States with the Baltic region, Britain, France, Italy, the Middle East, India, and China. Economic or political upheaval in one region affected its partners in commerce. The global economy moved more slowly before the era of instant communications, but international trade was an important factor in American lives. Most households below the most elite levels of society were involved intimately in some aspect of textile production or distribution. Textiles—and the products made from them, including samplers and other girlhood embroideries—were valued very differently than they are today.

Samplers are so much more than the quaint record of a girl's training in the female arts. In the web of these pieces of cloth are stories that help us understand how the makers of these samplers lived their lives, what influenced their thoughts and guided their actions, where and by whom they were educated, which customs were observed or shattered, and what viewpoints were taken. Kathleen Staples, guest curator of the exhibition *Georgia's Girlhood Embroidery: "Crowned with Glory and Immortality,"* has crafted in this volume a journey through the history of Georgia's young sampler makers, opening to us new perspectives on stories as disparate as Georgia's colonial sericulture experiments and Revolutionary War pension claims. Through her detailed research, Staples revitalizes our understanding of these textiles as documents and our appreciation of them as objects of admiration.

Madelyn Shaw, *Curator of Textiles, Division of Home and Community, National Museum of American History, Smithsonian Institution*

PREFACE

The study of girlhood embroideries made in southern states is a relatively new field. Until the late twentieth century, sampler making was presumed to be a northern practice. This assumption started, in part, because serious needlework scholarship began earlier in the North, taking root in the 1920s in New England. Thus, a great deal of study was undertaken and published on the tangible fruits of colonial and antebellum girlhood education in New England, Pennsylvania, and the mid-Atlantic states. Although both individuals and museums assembled collections of southern embroidery throughout the twentieth century, the provenance of many of these artifacts has remained elusive; some examples have been misidentified, making scholarly research difficult. Furthermore, some percentage of southern women's handwork has disappeared for reasons complicated by the isolation of rural communities, cultural preferences and traditions, lost kinship ties across generations, and the disruptive circumstances brought about by the Revolutionary and Civil Wars.

In 1972, the Museum of Early Southern Decorative Arts in Winston-Salem, North Carolina, began collecting and setting standards for documenting southern decorative arts, including textiles and needlework, of the colonial and antebellum periods. In-depth scholarship on southern embroideries went public with a series of exhibitions and accompanying catalogues, beginning with Betty Whiting Flemming's regional Virginia study *Threads of History: A Sampler of Girlhood Embroidery, 1792–1860, Loudoun County Area* (1995); followed by *In the Neatest Manner: The Making of the Virginia Sampler Tradition* (Kim Smith Ivey, 1997); *This Have I Done: Samplers and Embroideries from Charleston and the Lowcountry* (Jan Hiester and Kathleen Staples, 2001); *Virtue Leads and Grace Reveals: Embroideries and Education in Antebellum South Carolina* (Pat Veasey, 2003); and *A Maryland Sampling: Girlhood Embroidery, 1738–1860* and *Columbia's Daughters: Girlhood Embroidery from the District of Columbia* by Gloria Seaman Allen (2007 and 2012, respectively). Additionally, in 2004, the Tennessee Sampler Survey was founded as a nonprofit organization to document samplers from that state and post them online (www.tennesseesamplers.com). These two decades of southern scholarship have demonstrated that the embroidery training and educational experiences of young girls in southern climes varied by geography as well as over time.

It was in this scholarly context that Ashley Callahan, then curator of decorative arts at the Georgia Museum of Art, and Dale Couch, then senior archivist at the Georgia Archives, began to document and record Georgia samplers. This project was born more than a decade ago when Callahan and Couch fused their notes to create files of known Georgia samplers, awaiting a time when the museum would be able to organize a seminal exhibition. The museum's Henry D. Green Center for the Study of the Decorative Arts maintains numerous sources that informed this important undertaking. Couch, with the encouragement of Dr. William Underwood Eiland, director of the Georgia Museum of Art, requested that I undertake the role of co-curator of this exhibition and chief author of the accompanying catalogue.

Georgia's girlhood work has yet to be fully illuminated: the embroideries featured in this exhibition catalogue are samplers in search of their stories. When studied in conjunction with primary sources—newspaper notices, diaries and letters, court and other legal documents—that survive from the colonial and antebellum periods, these objects enrich our understanding of Georgia's settlement, both in-migration and out-migration; the influence of religion on female education; the consequences of economic growth; and personal disaster. Georgia's embroideries are visual narratives of kinship ties, business interests, and the flow of people, goods, and ideas across regional boundaries.

This catalogue, and the exhibition it accompanies, is not intended to be a definitive study of Georgia's girlhood embroidery, but the event and publication offer ground-breaking research to inspire and encourage further documentation, investigation, and conservation of these southern textile treasures.

Objects in the Catalogue

The embroideries in this catalogue come from a variety of sources: some descended in the families of the makers; others are cared for by discerning collectors; yet others are in the collections of southern museums.

Except where noted, all the embroideries were executed as counted techniques. That is, the alphabets, numbers, inscriptions, and designs were not drawn onto the fabric first. The worker counted the threads of the ground fabric to execute each stitch. She may have copied elements such as alphabets, numbers, and simple border designs from another sampler—one worked by her instructor or by a family member or friend. Decorative motifs and borders with more complex colorways may have been copied or adapted from published pattern sources.

Language, Places, and Dates

Language can be problematic when using primary sources. In order to preserve their original tone, all quotes from primary sources retain their archaic spellings, capitalization and punctuation, and use of italics. In this publication, the word "negro," the use of which is anathema today, is present only in period quotations; these describe either an enslaved runaway or an individual who is to be sold. During the period covered in the text, indigenous peoples of the Americas did not have a single term for themselves. Today many indigenous peoples accept the terms "Indian," "American Indian," or "Native People" (the preferred collective is nation rather than tribe). Despite questions about the possible political correctness of these words, all are used interchangeably in the text.

Unless specified, all of the counties mentioned in the text are in Georgia.

Life, marriage, and death dates for needleworkers and their family members are based on information from United States Federal Census records, county death records, certified court testimony, family bibles, and headstones and other data found on the genealogical and historical record websites Fold3.com and Ancestry.com.

Kathleen Staples, *independent scholar and guest curator*

ACKNOWLEDGMENTS

In 2015, the National Endowment for the Arts recognized the scholarly merit of this project and we acknowledge with great appreciation its financial support. We are grateful, as well, to Howard and Helen Elkins, who provided funding. We also thank Robert and Suzanne Currey for their generous support early on, and for their friendship and encouragement.

It would have been impossible to produce this catalogue without the assistance and cooperation of the following individuals and institutions. We are enormously grateful to the exhibition's lenders: Judge Eugene and Christie Benton, Roger and Cindy Bregenzer, and Carole Carpenter Wahler; the Charleston Museum, Charleston, South Carolina; James K. Polk Home and Museum, Columbia, Tennessee; the Midway Museum, Midway, Georgia, the Museum of Early Southern Decorative Arts (MESDA), Winston-Salem, North Carolina; the National Archives and Records Administration (NARA), Washington, DC; St. Vincent's Academy, Savannah, Georgia; Telfair Museums, Savannah, Georgia; and one anonymous private lender. In addition, the Colonial Williamsburg Foundation provided an image of its Georgia sampler (Letitia Malvina Mills), which was unavailable for loan, and Kimberly Smith Ivey, curator of textiles and historic interiors, DeWitt Wallace Decorative Arts Museum, Colonial Williamsburg Foundation, graciously shared her research and documentation of this embroidery for the catalogue entry.

A number of institutions and individuals were particularly helpful with primary source research and the examination of objects: Ashley Callahan, former curator of decorative arts at the Georgia Museum of Art; Jane Fitzgerald, archivist and vault manager, and James Zeender, exhibits registrar, at NARA; the staff of the Georgia Historical Society; Grant Gerlich, archivist, Mercy Heritage Center, Sisters of Mercy of the Americas, Belmont, North Carolina; the staff of the Manuscript, Archives, and Rare Book Library, Emory University, Atlanta; Sharen Lee, librarian at the Georgia Room, Bull Street Library, Savannah; curator Tania Sammons and administrative assistant Cyndi Sommers, Telfair Museums; Sister Jude Walsh and Loretto Lominack, St. Vincent's Academy; executive director Dianne Kroell and secretary and past chairperson of the Midway Museum Board of Governors Tina M. Scott at the Midway Museum; and historians and genealogists Mary Bondurant Warren and Mary Anne Hoit Abbe.

As with any large project, numerous individuals contributed crucial assistance. We wish to thank the entire staff at the Georgia Museum of Art, especially grant writer Betty Alice Fowler, registrar Christy Sinksen, and editor Stella Tran. The Henry D. Green Center for the Study of the Decorative Arts is staffed in part by student interns. Three interns, Joseph Litts, Caroline Rainey, and Rebecca Stapleford, provided ongoing assistance with this project. Athenian Margie Spalding was instrumental in locating a "lost" needlework. Others to whom we owe a debt of gratitude include Robert Leath, Daniel Ackermann, Graham Long, Laree Benton, and Margie Kelly. Thanks are also extended to the Georgia Museum of Art's Decorative Arts Advisory Committee and its chair, Linda Crowe Chesnut, for their support in this and other exhibitions at the museum. The director of the museum, Dr. William Underwood Eiland, provided enthusiastic support for this project from its inception.

We extend a special thank you to Jenny Garwood, researcher at MESDA, for her insightful catalogue entry on the Mary Smallwood sampler.

Finally, this project would not have been possible without the patience and support of family and friends and Joe J. Ashley, Gregory K. Jarrell, and Madelyn Shaw.

Kathleen Staples, *independent scholar and guest curator*

Dale Couch, *Curator of Decorative Arts, Henry D. Green Center for the Study of the Decorative Arts, Georgia Museum of Art*

Samuel Augustus Mitchell, map of Georgia, 1860. Courtesy of the David Rumsey Map Collection through a Creative Commons License.

A NEW MAP OF THE STATE OF GEORGIA EXHIBITING ITS INTERNAL IMPROVEMENTS Roads Distances &c.
BY J.H. YOUNG
PHILADELPHIA: PUBLISHED BY
CHARLES DESILVER 714 Chesnut St.
SCALE OF MILES
5 10 20 30 40 50
EXPLANATION
State Capital
County Towns
Common do.
Railroads
Do. in progress
Longitude West from Washington
Longitude West from Greenwich
TENNESSEE
N. CAROLINA
SOUTH CAROLINA
ALABAMA
FLORIDA
ATLANTIC OCEAN
TALLAHASSEE
Apalachee Bay
St. Marks
Newport
Port Leon
Jacksonville
Cumberland Sound
Fernandina
Amelia Island
Cumberland Island
St. Andrews Sound
St. Simons Sound
Altamaha Sound
Sapelo Sound
Ossabaw
Wassaw
Edgefield C.H.
Aiken
Barnwell C.H.
Anderson C.H.
Pickens C.H.
Abbeville
Columbus
Chattahoochee
Muscogee
Stewart
Randolph
Early
Baker
Decatur
Thomas
Lowndes
Clinch
Ware
Camden
Wayne
Glynn
McIntosh
Liberty
Bryan
Bulloch
Tatnall
Appling
Montgomery
Telfair
Irwin
Pulaski
Dooly
Sumter
Lee
Dougherty
Worth
Colquitt
Berrien
Miller
Calhoun
Terrell
Marion
Macon
Houston
Twiggs
Wilkinson
Laurens
Emanuel
Scriven
Effingham
Burke
Jefferson
Washington
Hancock
Baldwin
Putnam
Jasper
Jones
Bibb
Monroe
Crawford
Taylor
Talbot
Harris
Upson
Pike
Meriwether
Troup
Heard
Coweta
Fayette
Henry
Butts
Spalding
Newton
Morgan
Greene
Taliaferro
Warren
Columbia
Richmond
Wilkes
Lincoln
Elbert
Oglethorpe
Clarke
Walton
Gwinnett
De Kalb
Cobb
Paulding
Polk
Floyd
Cass
Cherokee
Forsyth
Hall
Jackson
Madison
Franklin
Hart
Habersham
Rabun
Union
Lumpkin
Gilmer
Pickens
Gordon
Murray
Whitfield
Walker
Dade
Chattooga
Haralson
Carroll
Campbell
Fulton
Jefferson
Waynesville
Thomasville
Bainbridge
Albany
Macon
Milledgeville
Augusta
Savannah
Atlanta

NEEDLEWORK and Female Education in Colonial and Antebellum Georgia

In contrast to the high-style embroidery worked by professional men and women in the textile trades, which has survived as ornamentation on historic apparel and soft furnishings, embroidered samplers are instructional exercises usually undertaken by young girls, in general, between the ages of eight and twelve. The content of surviving samplers from Georgia's colonial and antebellum periods ranges from rows of alphabets with inscriptions in prose and verse to architecture and decorative floral borders. Because a sampler generally included alphabets, sampler-making also was referred to, especially in newspaper advertisements, as marking. In use since at least the sixteenth century in England, the term "marking" identified the process of embroidering initials on household linens and linen undergarments to identify ownership (these initials were especially useful when objects were sent to be laundered). For at least some of their makers, a sampler was just one of a series of needlework experiments that might have included seam construction, mending, knitting, tambour work, and silk embroidery.

Newspaper advertisements, journal entries, and letters dating to Georgia's colonial and antebellum periods all reveal that the acquisition of needlework skills took place in a variety of settings: public and private, elective and required, urban and rural. The students themselves represented almost all levels of society, from orphaned and economically disadvantaged girls to the daughters of Georgia's most successful merchants and planters.

Orphan and Charity Schools

Orphan and charity schools provided settings in which white girls who found themselves without proper guardianship could be trained to the needle. The first such institution in Georgia was the orphan house in the village of Ebenezer. Ebenezer was established in 1733 by a group of German Lutheran settlers originally from Salzburg, Germany, who had fled their homeland because of religious persecution.[1] In exchange for resettlement in the colony, London's Georgia Board of Trustees offered these Salzburgers free transportation, land, maintenance until their first crops were raised, the right to practice their own language and religion, and the full rights of English citizens. England's Society for Promoting Christian Knowledge supplied additional financial support and supplies. Ebenezer's ministers, Johann Martin Boltzius and Israel Christian Gronau, had been connected with a well-known and well-respected orphanage in Halle, Germany. Realizing the need for a similar resource to care for orphans and the children of poverty-stricken families in their new settlement, Boltzius and Gronau raised funds for an orphan house, work on which began in 1737 and was completed early in 1738. In July of that year, the orphanage was supplied

. . . samplers are instructional exercises usually undertaken by young girls, in general, between the ages of eight and twelve.

with two spinning wheels, and in November, some of the orphan girls were spinning and knitting wool that Boltzius had purchased in Savannah, Georgia.[2] Although nothing textile-related is known to have survived, it is likely that these girls also learned basic sewing skills, including marking.

Inspired by the Ebenezer orphanage's care for its charges, English evangelist George Whitefield, with the help of Savannah schoolmaster James Habersham, established an orphanage on a five-hundred-acre tract about twelve miles south of Savannah.[3] In March of 1740, work began on the foundation for a main house. When completed, at the close of 1741, the newly named Bethesda Orphan House complex consisted of a two-story "great house" with a surrounding piazza, an infirmary, four framed houses, a large stable, and a cart house.[4] Whitefield reported at this time that among the girls at Bethesda were two or three who spun cotton and some who knitted; and "all that are capable, are taught to sew."[5] One of the first wards of the orphanage was twelve-year-old Sarah Gibb, a South Carolina orphan with an estate valued at 200 British pounds. By 1743, she was employed "at school, and needle work."[6]

The Savannah Free School was founded in 1816 for the purpose of educating the children—girls as well as boys—of impoverished parents. The school adopted a monitorial system of education developed by England's Joseph Lancaster (1778–1838). Under this system, older and more accomplished students taught younger, less advanced ones. In this way, a large number of students with varying skill levels could be taught in one place. The teacher monitored the classroom activities and assisted the student instructors as needed. For the girls' curriculum, Lancaster's sister, Mary, created a progressive, systematic plan for teaching practical needlework and produced a manual, *Origins of the Lancasterian System of Tuition for Females*; a Baltimore, Maryland, edition was published in 1821. The lessons, which involved creating actual specimens of work, were organized by degree of technical difficulty, with emphasis on basic

Figure 1. Engraving of a marking sampler to be used as a guide in the production of a diminutive sampler for the "Twelfth Class Work," *Origins of the Lancasterian System of Tuition for Females*. Baltimore, ca. 1821. Image courtesy Maryland Historical Society.

TWELFTH CLASS WORK.

Marking.

Figure 14th.

Various specimens of samplers might be exhibited, but the annexed plate represents one containing the large and small alphabet and figures, up to twelve, are sufficient attainments to prepare a child for marking of linen, or practising on samplers at length.

The pupils who are in this class, first mark on very wide and coarse canvass, so that they may see the threads, and easily count the stitches; after sufficient practice, they mark on finer materials.

sewing skills and the construction of diminutive versions of ordinary articles of dress. The twelfth lesson was a marking sampler (fig. 1).

The Savannah Free School's governing board initially searched for a teacher from New York who was familiar with the Lancasterian system. These efforts failed, but the board was able to engage by contract a Mr. Adams and his daughter, who must have agreed to implement Lancaster's methods. They arrived from Boston in December of 1817. Adams reported to the board on April 1, 1818, that several of the female students "have . . . gone nearly through a course of Class lessons in Sewing." In the next several months, some of the student seamstresses constructed full-size plain garments that were sold to the general public.[7] Miss Adams continued to instruct the girls until 1821. Surviving records for the school (which end with the destruction of the building in a fire on June 6, 1852) indicate that attracting teachers familiar with the Lancasterian system remained a challenge for the school's administrators for more than three decades.

Tutors

A wealthy planter might have hired a tutor to instruct either at his plantation house or residence in town. Reminiscing to his daughter about plantation life in Georgia when he was a boy, Charles Colcock Jones Jr. (1831–1893) noted that his father had engaged private tutors for himself and his brother and sister. Schoolhouses were built at Maybank and Montevideo, the Colcock family's two plantations in Liberty County: "At the former the children of our neighbor, Mr. Russell King, united with us, and at the latter were also convened the children of Mr. John Barnard."[8]

A teacher might advertise for a private position. For example, in 1822 a "single Lady, capable of teaching Reading, Writing, Arithmetic, Geography, Grammar, Drawing and Needlework" sought a position in a private family and had "no objections to go in the country, if in a healthy situation."[9] Two sisters from Charleston, "who do not wish to be separated," advertised their services for a private family or public institution "as Teachers for . . . Vocal Music, Guitar, Drawing, Needlework, Writing and Spelling." The special advantage of their employment was that "they require[d] the salary only of one person . . . [and] each can assist the other."[10]

A wealthy planter might have hired a tutor to instruct either at his plantation house or residence in town.

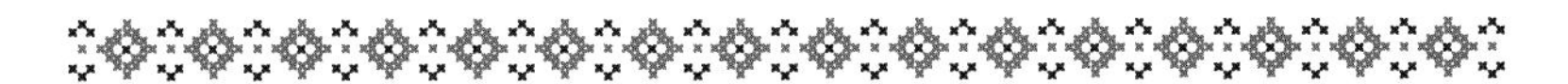

Some instructors were family members. In 1750, William Spencer wrote to the secretary of the Georgia Board of Trustees, Benjamin Martyn, to describe his experiences since arriving in the colony in 1742. He had settled at the town of Frederica on St. Simons Island only to lose everything in July of that year during an invasion by Spanish forces based in Florida (this action was part of the larger conflict known as the War of Jenkins' Ear). Among the casualties were his wife and two of his children. Spencer continued, "Upwards of Five Years ago (having two Young Daughters the Eldest about Nine Years old, who were in want of a proper Person to learn them how to live in the World)," he was fortunate to meet and marry "a sober discreet Woman." Since then, she had been "a good Step Mother to my said Daughters, having learnt them to be good House Wifes and also expert at their Needles."[11]

Elizabeth Lichtenstein Johnson (1764–1848), whose parents settled in Yamacraw, "in the suburbs of Savannah," recalled that she was early put to school.

When her mother died in 1774, Elizabeth was sent to live in Savannah with a maternal great aunt, a Mrs. Richard. She recollected:

> I attended the best schools in the place. My aunt did me every justice in bringing me up, and endeavored to make me a notable needlewoman, in which art she herself excelled, but my love for reading was so much greater than for sewing that I often had a book under my work to look into as opportunity offered. The good old lady not being able to make me perfect in sewing, declared at last that I should never be anything but a botcher at it, yet I did not think I really deserved the charge.[12]

When the Revolutionary War erupted, Elizabeth's father, Loyalist John Lichtenstein, escaped to Nova Scotia on a British man-of-war; father, daughter, and aunt were reunited when the British seized control of Savannah in 1778 (the British occupied the city until the end of the war). Elizabeth continued her education under her aunt's direction. She enjoyed the academic subjects but was loath to continue in the ornamental branches: "My aunt was kind, but was at the same time decided in her conduct toward me, and I was made industrious at my needle."[13]

Schools and Academies

Other forms of organized instruction were offered in both urban and rural settings to girls whose parents or guardians could afford the tuition—and boarding costs if required. Appendix D of this book lists eighty-seven teachers and academies advertising classes in sewing, needlework, and embroidery in Georgia between 1768 and 1848. There were no agreed-upon standards, and education for girls was not compulsory. Some instructors taught only reading, writing, and practical skills with a needle. Others offered expanded curricula that included plain needlework and fancy embroidery, academic subjects,

Some instructors taught only reading, writing, and practical skills with a needle. Others offered expanded curricula that included plain needlework and fancy embroidery, academic subjects, and dancing and music.

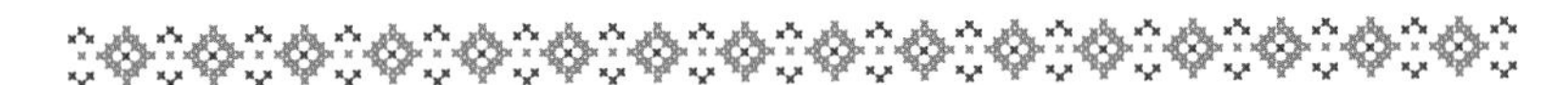

and dancing and music. A few teachers and institutions adopted a particular educational method, as exemplified by the aforementioned Savannah Free School's implementation of the Lancasterian system. In 1795, Thomas and Leah Sandwich advertised that their academy, Mount Salubrity, near Augusta, was run "upon the plan of Dr. Rush [Benjamin Rush] of Philadelphia." By 1804, Thomas, widowed and remarried, grounded his educational offerings "on the plan of Bethlehem," the Moravian school in Pennsylvania, having hired a tutor from that school.[14]

The first notice for female education in Georgia that included needlework instruction appeared in Savannah's *Georgia Gazette* in September of 1768. James Cosgreve advertised that he planned to open a school where academic subjects would be offered to "young Gentlemen and Ladies." At the conclusion of his notice, he added that his wife "would undertake to teach young Ladies to sew and read." By the close of the eighteenth century, at least fourteen married couples, widows, and single women advertised instruction in needlework near or in a Georgia town or village. In the first half of the nineteenth century, day schools, which offered little more than reading, writing, and plain needlework, were superseded by academies and boarding schools. The latter provided expanded curricula of academic subjects, foreign languages, and science, as well as the ornamental branches, which included more intricate forms of embroidery such as silkwork, ribbon work, flowering and tambour work, and Berlin work.

Education for African Americans

The presence of Africans and African Americans was not a marginal feature of girlhood education in the South. Gloria Seaman Allen has documented, from the antebellum era, Baltimore's Oblate Sisters' School for Colored Girls and Saint James's First African Protestant Episcopal Church School, both of which offered the daughters of unskilled laborers and domestic servants a curriculum that included needlework instruction.[15] I have previously demonstrated how, in the eighteenth century, some of the daughters of enslaved persons from Charleston, South Carolina, received a needlework education either through an apprenticeship system or by enrollment in the same formal and informal schools attended by white girls.[16] In the latter, teachers offered both segregated and integrated instruction.

Georgia's records have yet to reveal similarly detailed information about how enslaved women and free women of color acquired their needlework expertise. Newspaper advertisements, however, indicate that those skills were highly marketable. In 1764, a master sold several "Valuable Slaves," among whom were seamstresses "as good . . . as any in this province."[17] In 1790, a young woman was offered for sale, "a complete seamstress . . . as such will be recommended."[18] At least one enslaved servant was in the needlework trade, providing income for her master: "A Mulatto Wench named Binah, having led a city life in my employ, as a seamstress, for these twelve years past, refuses to retire into the country, and absconded yesterday morning."[19] Another runaway, Beckey, was "an excellent seamstress, and carried off with her some very good clothing."[20] As a final example, there is an advertisement, not for the sale, but for the hire of "a negro girl 11 or 12 years of age . . . she is careful, a little acquainted with needle work, and can card and spin."[21]

In 1823, the *Augusta Chronicle* printed a list of free persons of color who had been required to register in Richmond County under an act "prescribing the mode of manumitting slaves in this state."[22] In addition to age, place of birth, and residence, registrants gave their occupations. Of the fifty-five women ages fifteen or older who were employed, forty-two of them listed themselves as part- or full-time seamstresses.

The firsthand account of former slave Susie Baker, born in 1848 in Liberty County and raised by her grandmother in Savannah, hints at the possibility of a clandestine education.[23] Susie received her first formal instruction in reading and writing from a free woman of color, joining a group of about twenty-five or thirty black children: "The [white] neighbors would see us going in sometimes, but they supposed we were there learning trades."[24] After two years of instruction there, her grandmother sent her to a Mrs. Mary Beasley to continue her education. A Confederate gunboat commander questioned Susie when she was twelve years old on whether she could read, write, and sew: "On hearing I could, he asked me to hem some napkins for him. He was surprised at my accomplishments."[25]

Out-of-State Educational Opportunities

Not all of Georgia's daughters received an education within the state. For various reasons, some parents and guardians chose to send girls abroad for formal training in the academic and ornamental branches. Some of these institutions were religious centers as well. Families with friendship or kinship ties in the North, those who sent their sons to northern colleges, and those who traveled to New England and the mid-Atlantic states all had opportunities to acquaint themselves with schools and academies in those areas that catered to female education. In the antebellum era, some establishments took the initiative to advertise in Georgia's newspapers. Esther and Elizabeth Scribner announced their day and boarding school located in Morristown, New Jersey, recommending its "cheapness of the terms of Tuition and the convenience of the distance from New-York." Academic subjects were supplemented with ornamental subjects, including "plain Sewing, Marking, elegant work upon Muslins, and Needle work of every description; with Embroidery."[26] A Mrs. Bartlette and a Miss Barnum ran the Young Ladies Academy in the "centre of the village" of Jamaica, on Long Island.[27] This trustee-administered school included two gentlemen from Savannah on its board. In 1831, a Miss E. Marcelly advertised her Academy for the Instruction of Young Ladies at No. 11, South Charles Street, in Baltimore. The course of instruction embraced plain and ornamental needlework. School discipline was mild, "firm and regular," and students' successes were rewarded with annual premiums.[28] In Philadelphia, a teaching order of sisters, les Dames de la Retraite, opened an academy on the French model: French was to be the exclusive language of the school, except in classes of English studies.[29] Included in the curriculum were lessons in fancy and ornamental needlework, presumably given in French.

Enrollment records of several out-of-state schools survive, providing names and allowing modern scholars to explore relationships among the girls and the nature of their education.

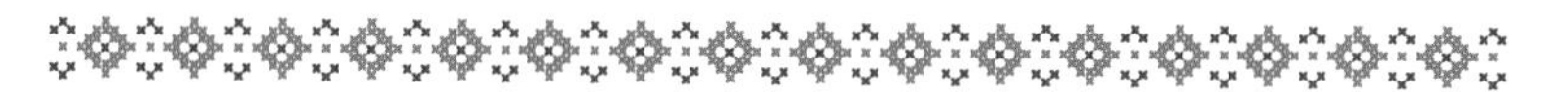

Closer to home, some of South Carolina's educational establishments also vied for Georgia's patronage. All of the following schools and teachers included needlework in their respective curricula. As early as the 1760s, some teachers produced handbills; one from a Mrs. Stokes's boarding school in Charleston was wrapped around some pound notes stolen from a house in Savannah.[30]

A Miss Thurston from England set up a boarding school for young ladies on William Scarbrough's seven-thousand-acre Belfast Plantation in Allendale County, South Carolina.[31] (Scarbrough was a successful shipping merchant and financier who split his time between Belfast and Savannah.) In 1824, the Columbia Female Academy, a trustee-administered boarding school, advertised in the *Milledgeville Journal* and *Augusta Chronicle* in Georgia as well as Alabama's *Mobile Commercial Register*.[32] A Mr. and Mrs. Lockwood advertised their South Carolina school, which likely received young boys as well as girls, in both Savannah and Augusta in 1830.[33] The female academy in Edgefield, South Carolina, boasted, in 1837, that it had engaged a new teacher, educated at New York's Troy Female Seminary.[34]

Enrollment records of several out-of-state schools survive, providing names and allowing modern scholars to explore relationships among the girls and the nature of their education.[35] Between 1785 and 1860, the Moravian Seminary for Young Ladies at Bethlehem, Pennsylvania, enrolled one hundred of Georgia's daughters, some of them siblings or cousins and, undoubtedly, the acquaintances or friends of others (see Appendix A).[36] The seminary offered a Christian education grounded in "the useful branches of learning, to the exclusion of all vain and frivolous accomplishments." Pupils learned the basics of plain sewing and knitting; the seminary introduced tambour and "fine needle work" in the fall of 1787, but required an additional fee.[37]

Litchfield Female Academy in Connecticut received twenty-one girls from Georgia between 1802 and 1830. Almost all of these students came from coastal communities—Savannah, Midway, Sunbury, Darien, and St. Marys (see Appendix B).[38] Founded by Sarah Pierce (b. 1767) in 1792 and active until 1833, the school could boast that more than 80 percent of its students came from out of town. Litchfield was known for its Congregational religious practice, which would have appealed to Midway and Sunbury families.

Margaret Eliza Clark, from St. Marys, Georgia, attended the academy from 1824 to 1825; her brother Henry attended in 1824. Their parents were Rhoda Wadsworth of Litchfield, a former Litchfield Academy student, and Archibald Bellinger Clark, who had graduated from the Litchfield Law School in 1800. Both children boarded with their grandparents to attend school.[39] The enrollment records also list Mary Jones Glen, from Savannah, who enrolled in 1802. Mary was the daughter of sampler maker Sarah Jones (see catalogue number 2) and John Glen.

As there was no standardized curriculum, a student learned only what her instructor—family member, neighbor, or paid teacher—was accomplished enough to teach and whose proficiency was limited to the extent of personal desire and talent.

North Carolina's Raleigh Academy must have been held in regard. In 1817, the *Reflector*, the main newspaper of Milledgeville, Georgia (the state's capital between 1804 and 1868), reported on the public examination of students at the academy in November, citing that one of four young graduates was Ann W. Clark of Georgia, who received "an Honorary Certificate on parchment and a Golden Medal."[40] In 1823, Susan Davis Nye, the head of the female department at Raleigh, resigned her position and moved to Augusta, Georgia, to open a female school. Her newspaper advertisements of that year noted her previous employment as "Late Principal Preceptress of the Female department of the Academy at Raleigh" and her intention to adapt the system of instruction "so successfully pursued" there.[41] Features of that education were "an honorary certificate and golden medal, with suitable device and inscriptions" given to students who finished their course of studies.[42]

The preceding discussions offer just an introduction to the diverse educational situations in which girls and young women of Georgia, enslaved and free, acquired skills in sewing, needlework, and embroidery. As there was no standardized curriculum, a student learned only what her instructor—family member, neighbor, or paid teacher—was accomplished enough to teach; proficiency was limited by personal desire and talent. For orphans, girls from humble circumstances, and free females of color, the acquisition of needlework skills could mean paid employment. Georgia's slave owners seem to have valued enslaved women who possessed these skills, but more research is needed to determine to what extent enslaved seamstresses used needle and thread to purchase their freedom. And for the daughters of Georgia's citizens, during most of the antebellum period, a school or academy education—complete with lessons in the ornamental branches—was de rigueur in polite society.

Kathleen Staples

NOTES

1. For an overall discussion of the Salzburger settlement in Georgia, see George Fenwick Jones, *The Georgia Dutch: From the Rhine and Danube to the Savannah, 1733–1783* (Athens: University of Georgia, 1992).
2. George Fenwick Jones and Renate Wilson, trans. and ed., *Detailed Reports on the Salzburger Emigrants Who Settled in America . . . Edited by Samuel Urlsperger*, vol. 5, *1738* (Athens: University of Georgia Press, 1980), 154 and 268.
3. For an overall discussion of the establishment and development of Bethesda Orphan House, see Erwin C. Surrency, "Whitefield, Habersham, and the Bethesda Orphanage," *Georgia Historical Quarterly* 34, no. 2 (June 1950): 87–105.
4. George Whitefield, *The Works of the Reverend George Whitefield*, vol. 3 (London, 1771), 433.
5. Ibid., 432.
6. *South-Carolina Gazette* (Charleston, SC), July 4, 1743.
7. Savannah Free School Society, MS 0689 vol. 1, Rules of the Society 1816–1838, Georgia Historical Society, Savannah, Georgia.
8. Robert Manson Myers, *Children of Pride: A True Story of Georgia and the Civil War* (New Haven, CT: Yale University, 1972), 19–20.
9. *Georgian* (Savannah, GA), July 25, 1822.
10. *Savannah (GA) Daily Republican*, October 11, 1843.

11. Savannah, July 18, 1750. *The Colonial Records of the State of Georgia,* vol. 26 (Atlanta: State of Georgia, 1916), 6–7.
12. Elizabeth Lichtenstein Johnston, *Recollections of a Georgia Loyalist*, ed. Arthur Wentworth Eaton (New York: M. F. Mansfield, 1901), 43–44.
13. Ibid., 50–51.
14. *Augusta (GA) Chronicle*; April 25, 1795, and February 4, 1804.
15. See relevant discussions in chapter 13, Gloria Seaman Allen, *A Maryland Sampling: Girlhood Embroidery, 1738–1860* (Baltimore: Maryland Historical Society, 2007).
16. Kathleen Staples, "Samplers from Charleston, South Carolina," *The Magazine Antiques* 169, no. 3 (March 2006): 80–89.
17. *Georgia Gazette* (Savannah, GA), October 4, 1764.
18. Ibid., June 24, 1790.
19. *Savannah (GA) Republican; and Savannah Evening Ledger*, January 11, 1810.
20. *Augusta (GA) Chronicle*, September 6, 1826.
21. *Georgian* (Savannah, GA), October 27, 1829.
22. *Augusta (GA) Chronicle*, May 3, and June 11 and 12, 1823.
23. Susie King Taylor, *Reminiscences of My Life in Camp*, ed. Patricia W. Romero (1902; repr., New York: Markus Wiener, 1988).
24. Ibid., 29. The Georgia Slave Acts of 1829 and 1833 made it a crime to teach slaves to read and write.
25. Ibid., 33.
26. *Savannah (GA) Republican*, May 16, 1809.
27. *Georgian* (Savannah, GA), June 22, 1822.
28. Ibid., May 4, 1831.
29. Ibid., August 9, 1832.
30. *Georgia Gazette* (Savannah, GA), December 27, 1769.
31. *Savannah (GA) Republican*, December 19, 1816.
32. *Georgia Journal* (Milledgeville, GA), May 4, 1824.
33. *Georgian* (Savannah, GA), November 3, 1830, and *Augusta (GA) Chronicle*, November 6, 1830.
34. *Augusta (GA) Constitutionalist*, November 23, 1837.
35. Published records for the Society of Friends School at Westtown, Pennsylvania, and the Moravian school at Lititz, Pennsylvania, indicate that girls from Georgia did not attend these institutions. See Susanna Smedley, comp., *Catalog of Westtown through the Years: Officers, Students, and Others, Fifth Month 1799 to Fifth Month 1945* (Westtown, PA: Westtown Alumni Association, 1945); and Patricia Herr, *"The Ornamental Branches": Needlework and Arts from the Lititz Moravian Girls' School between 1800 and 1865* (Lancaster, PA: Heritage Center of Lancaster County, 1996).
36. The Moravian Seminary was one of three American Moravian schools. The other two are in Lititz, Pennsylvania, and Winston-Salem, North Carolina. See William C. Reichel and William H. Bigler, *A History of the Rise, Progress, and Present Condition of the Moravian Seminary for Young Ladies, at Bethlehem, Pa., with a Catalogue of Its Pupils, 1785–1858 . . . with a Continuation of the History and Catalogue to the Year 1870*, 2nd ed. (Philadelphia: J. B. Lippincott, 1874), 334–505.
37. Ibid., 37–38 and 41.
38. "Students Known to Have Attended the Litchfield Female Academy," in Catherine Keene Fields and Lisa C. Kightlinger, eds., *To Ornament Their Minds: Sarah Pierce's Litchfield Female Academy, 1792–1833* (Litchfield, CT: Litchfield Historical Society, 1993), 115–31.

39. Lynne Templeton Brickley, "Sarah Pierce's Litchfield Female Academy," in Fields and Kightlinger, 30.
40. *Milledgeville (GA) Reflector*, December 2, 1817.
41. *Augusta Chronicle* and *Georgia Advertiser*, June 28 and September 20, 1823. For a discussion of Susan Nye's life and work, see Kim Tolley and Margaret A. Nash, "Leaving Home to Teach: The Diary of Susan Nye Hutchison, 1815–1841," in *Chartered Schools: Two Hundred Years of Independent Academies in the United States, 1727–1925*, ed. Nancy Beadie and Kim Tolley (New York: Routledge, 2013), 161–85.
42. *Augusta Chronicle and Georgia Advertiser*, December 20, 1823.

her sampler she
was born in the year of our lord
1775
Bonner Her Sampler
She was Born The 8 Day of january in the
year 1775 And also married the 20 Day of
December 1792 to Mr John McKenzie
James Bonner was Born the patsey McKenzie
2 Day of December
was B

Martha MCKENZIE

In the fall of 1846, Martha (Patsey) Bonner McKenzie traveled more than a hundred miles from her home in Carroll County, Tennessee, to visit her daughter Nancy and family in Lafayette County, Mississippi.[1] Now seventy-one years old and a widow, Martha had lost her husband, John McKenzie, almost four years previously, in November of 1842. John had farmed in Tennessee for twenty-six years, from 1816 (when the family moved from Washington County to Maury County, Tennessee) until his death. Even as an octogenarian—although with the help of four adult slaves—he worked the Carroll County land the McKenzie family had settled on in 1828. Making ends meet had not been so difficult in those final years. Beginning in 1835, John received an annual pension of $480 for his service in the Revolutionary War.[2]

The payments had stopped shortly after John's death. In 1843, with the help of the couple's eldest son, Jeremiah, who lived in neighboring Gibson County, Martha applied for a Revolutionary War widow's pension.[3] She testified at the Carroll County court that she did not have a copy of the marriage license, nor could she obtain one because "at the time of her marriage that part of Georgia [Washington County] was on the frontier and not many of the counties organized, and she supposes the record has been lost or destroyed." She mentioned that she still possessed a sample of needlework on which she had embroidered the date of her marriage. Her sons Jeremiah and Alexander swore that John and Martha McKenzie were their parents. Emily McKenzie Gilbert, Martha's sister-in-law, stated that she had not attended the wedding because she was at her brother's house arranging the "a-fair" that was to take place the next day.

Embroidered sampler worked by Martha "Patsey" Bonner McKenzie (1775–1851); two dates of completion: ca. 1785 and 1792. Worked possibly in Virginia and in Washington County, Georgia. Two-ply silk thread; balanced plain weave linen consists of three small pieces sewn together prior to execution of embroidery. Stitches: counted cross over 2 x 2 threads, square eyelet over 4 x 4 threads; surface chain. 11 5/16 x 10 1/8 inches. National Archives and Records Administration, Washington, DC

She testified at the Carroll County court that she did not have a copy of the marriage license, nor could she obtain one. . . . She mentioned that she still possessed a sample of needlework on which she had embroidered the date of her marriage.

When John brought Martha home with him, he introduced her as his bride.[4] Apparently none of this testimony satisfied the pension office of the War Department in Washington, DC, that Martha was the lawful wife of John McKenzie. Her application was denied.

In October 1846, Martha was prepared to go to court again, not in Tennessee but in Mississippi. Leaving her daughter's home in Oxford, she traveled about sixty miles to Hernando, in DeSoto County. There, on the twenty-sixth, she presented herself before Justice David J. White to "obtain the benefit of the provisions made by the acts of Congress . . . granting . . . . Pensions to certain widows." After describing her husband's military service, she admitted (as she had done in 1843) that she had "no documentary or record proof in support of her claim." She once again brought up her embroidered sampler, which she called "an old work sample." She elaborated that the sample, which "she had previous to her marriage," "contains the precise date of her marriage to the Said John McKenzie" as well as her own date of birth, all "worked with a needle in letters and figures." She explained that she had stitched the wedding date "but a few weeks after she was married."[5]

Sympathetic to Martha's situation, Justice White himself gave sworn testimony in support of her claim. He noted that he was well acquainted with the applicant, "a woman of truth and veracity." He argued that she suffered from "old Age and bodily infirmity," and for this reason, she had not attended the Carroll County courthouse to make this new application.[6]

It is notable—and likely part of a coordinated effort on the part of mother and son—that three days before Martha's appearance before Justice White, Jeremiah stood before Justice Rufus King in Gibson County, Tennessee. Jeremiah testified about his father's receipt of a pension; family records kept by his father, which were accidentally destroyed by fire; and Martha's previous application for a pension. Most important, he remembered "distinctly seeing his mother Patsey McKenzie have an old worked sample upon which she has the date of her marage worked in with a needle which sample . . . [he] has frequently seen in his mother's possession from his earliest recollection and has often heard her say that she was at work on said sample at the time she was married to . . . John McKenzie."[7]

The climax to these events was the appearance of Martha's youngest son, James, before Justice Needham Green in Carroll County on November 3.[8] He produced Martha's "old worked sample," which he had known about since childhood and "which Contains as this aplicant has always understood the date of the marriage of his Father and Mother."[9] Along with James's sworn testimony, Justice Green took the embroidered sampler into evidence.

With this action, a textile became a text. The embroidery was accepted as a valid document and added to John McKenzie's pension file at the War Department. Martha was issued a certificate of pension on December 15, 1846. She received $200 per year from that time until March 1848, after which the amount was increased to $480, and then to $600 in 1850.[10]

Although her testimony is unclear on this point, Martha likely constructed and embroidered most of her modest sampler as a young girl—sometime

With this action, a textile became a text. The embroidery was accepted as a valid document and added to John McKenzie's pension file at the War Department.

between 1783 and 1787—in either Virginia or Georgia.[11] The 1850 federal census indicates that she was born in Virginia, but it is not known when she moved to Georgia and her parents have yet to be identified. She was in Washington County, Georgia, however, by 1792, the year of her marriage. The sampler linen comprises three small rectangles of fabric that she hemmed and carefully slip stitched together at their edges before commencing the embroidery. Divided into three wide panels, the embroidery itself is overwhelmingly alphabets and inscriptions. The only decorative elements are two narrow horizontal bands of a wavy pattern that resemble rows of irish stitch—which creates a flamelike pattern when worked in rows of multiple colors—but are executed in chain stitch.[12]

The top panel of the sampler is distinguished by alphabets and numerals. Martha was apparently intrigued by the different ways in which the letter W could be executed in counted stitches. She recorded four variations of the letter in her uppercase alphabet and worked five larger versions in a separate row. The middle panel records her nickname, surname, and initials: "Patsy Bonner" and "PB" as well as her birth year, 1775.

The information crucial to Martha's pension application appears in the bottom panel. In addition to a restatement of her birth information (which she might have stitched as a young girl or inserted at the time of her marriage), she recorded her marriage date, December 20, 1792, and the name of her spouse, "Mr. John McKenzie." Apparently as an afterthought, she stitched her brother's name, James Bonner. She perhaps intended to stitch his full birth date, but completed only the day of his birth. The initials C.A.M. at bottom center have yet to be identified.

A note dated 1910 in John McKenzie's pension file records that Martha's sampler had been removed from a case and locked away in the Revolutionary War section of the Record Division. Her embroidery was not rediscovered until 1971, when the National Archives microfilmed the Revolutionary War pension records.

NOTES

1. Nancy Jane McKenzie Rounsaville (1805–1867).
2. The Revolutionary War service record of John H. McKenzie (1757–1842) is well documented in his pension file. A Virginia native, he served from 1776 to 1782 and took part in the following battles in Virginia and North and South Carolina: Rocky Mount, Hanging Rock, Camden, Rugley's Mills, Ironworks, Torrence's Tavern, Guilford, New Market, Beatties Ford, and Orangeburg. See Pension record W.1049, Revolutionary War Pension and Bounty-Land Application Files, National Archives and Records Administration (NARA), Fold3.com.
3. Jeremiah H. McKenzie (1793–1858).
4. Pension record W.1049. All of the affidavits were made October 3, 1843.
5. Ibid. Sworn testimony of Martha McKenzie.
6. Ibid. Sworn testimony of David J. White.
7. Ibid. Sworn testimony of Jeremiah H. McKenzie.
8. James Monroe McKenzie (1818–1873).
9. Pension record W.1049. Sworn testimony of James M. McKenzie.
10. Ibid. Martha M. Kenzie, Certificate of Pension; two untitled documents.
11. In colonial America, girls who indicated their ages in stitches were generally between eight and twelve.
12. The term "irish" does not refer to a geographic region. In use as a name for a specific embroidery pattern since the 1500s, irish is more likely related to the Greek *iris*, meaning rainbow. When successive rows of the stitch are worked in different colors, the effect can be iridescent.

No. 02

Sarah JONES

Sarah Jones was born into one of the great Georgia lineages. Her grandfather, Noble Jones (1702–1775), had arrived with James Oglethorpe in what was not yet the town of Savannah in February of 1733, on the first ship to carry English settlers to the newly established colony. Accompanying him were his wife, Sarah Hack Jones (born ca. 1703), and two children, Mary and Noble Wimberley (Sarah's father). Unlike most of the passengers aboard the *Anne*, Noble Jones, who was both a carpenter and a physician, had not needed the financial support of the Georgia Board of Trustees to make the journey. The family was given a house lot in Savannah, and Noble was granted large tracts of land in the Georgia low country over the ensuing years. In the late 1730s, he established a large plantation he called Wormslow (the spelling was changed to Wormsloe in the mid-nineteenth century), which served variously as a military stronghold, a plantation with diversified agricultural activities and an increasing adoption of bound labor, and an experimental laboratory for sericulture.[1]

Trained by his father as a physician, Noble Wimberly Jones (ca. 1723–1805) married Sarah Davis (ca. 1738–1815) of South Carolina in 1755. Their daughter Sarah, the sampler maker, was born the following year, and the marriage would eventually produce fourteen children. Thus, the household in which Sarah was raised was an increasingly active one: her father not only practiced medicine and continued to accumulate land and slaves, but also became involved in the politics of the colony as an ardent Whig.[2] By 1770, Noble Wimberly owned a five-hundred-acre plantation, three Savannah town lots, and twenty-eight slaves.[3]

Embroidered tablet-style sampler by Sarah Jones (ca. 1756–1804), dated July 1763. Worker's residence: Savannah, Christ Church Parish. Two-ply twisted silk thread on balanced plain weave linen. Left and right sides of sampler cannot be seen in frame; top and bottom edges turned under twice and hemmed. Stitches: counted cross over 1 x 1 and 2 x 2 threads; counted satin. 15 1/4 x 13 ½ inches. Collection of the Telfair Museum of Art, Gift of Mrs. Hubert Bond Owens. 1971.4

The Commandments
I
Adore no other Gods but only me
II
Worship not God by any thing you see
III
IIII
Let Sabbaths be a rest for men and beast
V
honour thy parent to prolong thy days
Our Father which
kingdom
as it
Heaven
this day
daily
and
trespasses as
them that
not into
But
Deliver us
Evil For
is
the
the
ever
Ten in Verse
VI
VII
VIII
IX
X
what may others damnify
in
Father
of Heaven
Earth
in Jesus Christ
was conceived by
Who
Virgin
under
was
and
into
Day
from
into
on
of
Fa
ther Almighty
he
the quick
in the
aged 7 years

It is not known where and under whose instruction Sarah made her sampler, but with the family residing in Savannah much of the time, Sarah, "aged 7 years," likely received instruction locally from a tutoress knowledgeable in creating elegant girlhood needlework in an English style. Sarah's sampler inscriptions—the Ten Commandments, the Lord's Prayer, and the Apostles' Creed—are the three chief parts, or backbone, of the Protestant catechism, and especially the Lutheran, Calvinist, and Anglican versions.[4] Sarah framed these summaries in a pair of elongated octagonal borders, reminiscent of both the Torah's description of Moses's two stone tablets inscribed with the "ten words" or the "ten sayings" (Exodus 20) and the religious texts carved into large tablets of wood or stone seen hanging on the walls of seventeenth- and eighteenth-century English Protestant churches.[5] Sarah's poetic text for the "Ten Commandments in Verse" was taken from *A Guide to the English Tongue in Two Parts* by English schoolmaster Rev. Thomas Dyche (d. ca. 1733; Mary Smallwood used the same verse; see catalogue number 3).[6] Dyche's verse was a popular poetic form for eighteenth- and early-nineteenth-century English sampler makers, many of whom framed the commandments in stitched, tablet-shaped borders:

I. Adore no other Gods but only me
II. Worship not God by any thing you see
III. Reverence Jehovahs name swear not in vain
IV. Let Sabbaths be a reast for man and beast
V. Honour thy parents to prolong thy days.
VI. Thou shalt not kill nor murdering quarrels raise.
VII. Adultry shun in chastity delight.
VIII. Thou shalt not steal nor take anothers right.
IX. In bearing witness never tell a lie.
X. Covet not what may others damnify.

Sarah's sampler inscriptions—the Ten Commandments, the Lord's Prayer, and the Apostles' Creed—are the three chief parts, or backbone, of the Protestant catechism

Sarah's Lord's Prayer ends with the phrase "for thine is the kingdom and the power and the glory for ever and ever Amen." This phrase, not recorded in the New Testament gospels of Matthew and Luke, is a doxology used particularly among Protestants. She ran out of space to complete the Apostles' Creed and finished abruptly with "the quick and the dead I believe in the Holy ghost."

In 1771, at about age fifteen, Sarah married attorney John Glen (1744–1799). Born in Charleston, South Carolina, and schooled in Philadelphia, Glen had moved to Savannah by 1768. As political rhetoric heated up in the aftermath of the Townsend and Stamp Acts and then the Intolerable Acts, Glen joined Georgians who actively supported colonial rights (this group included his father-in-law) and organized a provincial congress. Under the new revolutionary government, formed in 1776, Glen was elected Georgia's first chief justice. Following Savannah's surrender to the British in 1778, Glen fled the British, leaving his family, and relocated to Charleston. With Charleston's capitulation to the enemy in 1780, he was arrested and made a prisoner of war. He returned to Savannah and switched loyalties, renouncing his Whig sympathies and signing a British loyalty oath—actions taken undoubtedly in an attempt to preserve his property from seizure by the British. At this point, Sarah and the children likely were living apart from him, on family property outside the city (Sarah's father, Noble Wimberley Jones, was imprisoned by the British in St. Augustine, Florida).

It is not known where and under whose instruction Sarah made her sampler, but with the family residing in Savannah much of the time, Sarah, "aged 7 years," likely received instruction locally from a tutoress knowledgeable in creating elegant girlhood needlework in an English style.

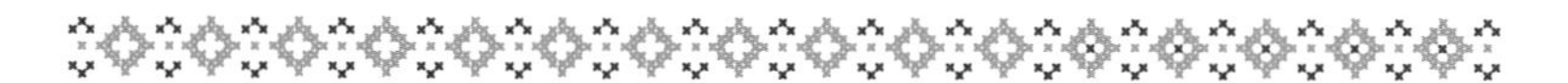

Peace brought recriminations against those who had supported the Loyalist cause. Glen's property was confiscated and auctioned, and he was banished from both Savannah and Charleston. Sarah and the children, however, remained in Savannah. She may have unofficially sided with her husband and father's politics or was under her father's protection; she certainly was receiving his aid and support and was allowed to travel without restrictions. In 1784, Sarah petitioned the Georgia Assembly. Although the circumstances of the event are unknown, she possibly appealed for financial amelioration and/or for leniency for her husband. In 1785, John Glen was restored to Georgia citizenship through Georgia's Act of Amercement: he was required to pay a special property tax and was barred from voting, holding office, and serving on juries for fourteen years. He eventually reacquired land and slaves and, in the 1790s, re-established his law practice. His political rehabilitation was complete when he was elected mayor of Savannah in 1797. Two years later he died of an unexplained illness, leaving Sarah with ten children.

According to letters written by her brother George and George's son Noble Wymberly, after her husband's death, Sarah traveled with family members to New York and New Jersey. She stayed at the house George owned in Middletown, Connecticut, on the Connecticut River.[7] About thirty miles away was the town of Litchfield, which boasted a law school and Sarah Pierce's Female Academy. Several of Sarah Jones's sons attended lectures at the law school, and in 1802, Sarah enrolled her daughter, Mary Jones Glen, in Sarah Pierce's school (see Appendix B). Suffering from consumption, Sarah died in September of 1804.[8]

Sarah Jones's sampler is the earliest known girlhood embroidery with a Georgia provenance. In 1921, Ethel Stanwood Bolton and Eva Johnston Coe documented the embroidery in their seminal survey, *American Samplers*.[9] The needlework descended from Sarah's daughter, Catherine Jones Glen Grimes, through a female line to the most recent owner, who then donated the sampler to Telfair Museums in 1971.

NOTES

1. Sarah's aunt, Mary Jones (ca. 1730–1795), in particular, took an active interest in silk production and became supervisor of the plantation's efforts. In 1751, the enterprise had produced six to eight ounces of silkworm eggs. See E. Merton Coulter, *Wormsloe: Two Centuries of a Georgia Family* (Athens: University of Georgia Press, 1955), 28.
2. For details on the political career of Noble Wimberly Jones, see *New Georgia Encyclopedia*, s.v. "Noble W. Jones," www.georgiaencyclopedia.org/articles/history-archaeology/noble-w-jones-ca-1723-1805.
3. Drew A. Swanson, *Remaking Wormsloe Plantation: The Environmental History of a Lowcountry Landscape* (Athens: University of Georgia Press, 2012), 35–36.
4. The Roman Catholic version includes a fourth summary, the Ave Maria.
5. In biblical Hebrew, the Ten Commandments are called the Aseret ha-Dibrot or D'varim.
6. First published in 1707 or 1709, this volume enjoyed many editions, the latest in 1830.
7. John Eddins Simpson, ed., *Jones Family Papers, 1760–1810*, Georgia Historical Society Collections, vol. 17 (Savannah: Georgia Historical Society, 1976). In the eighteenth century, Middletown was a thriving port, comparable to Boston or New York, and the trafficking of slaves was a large part of the town's economy.
8. Ibid., 26.
9. Ethel Stanwood Bolton and Eva Johnston Coe, *American Samplers* (1921; repr., New York: Weathervane, 1973), 57.

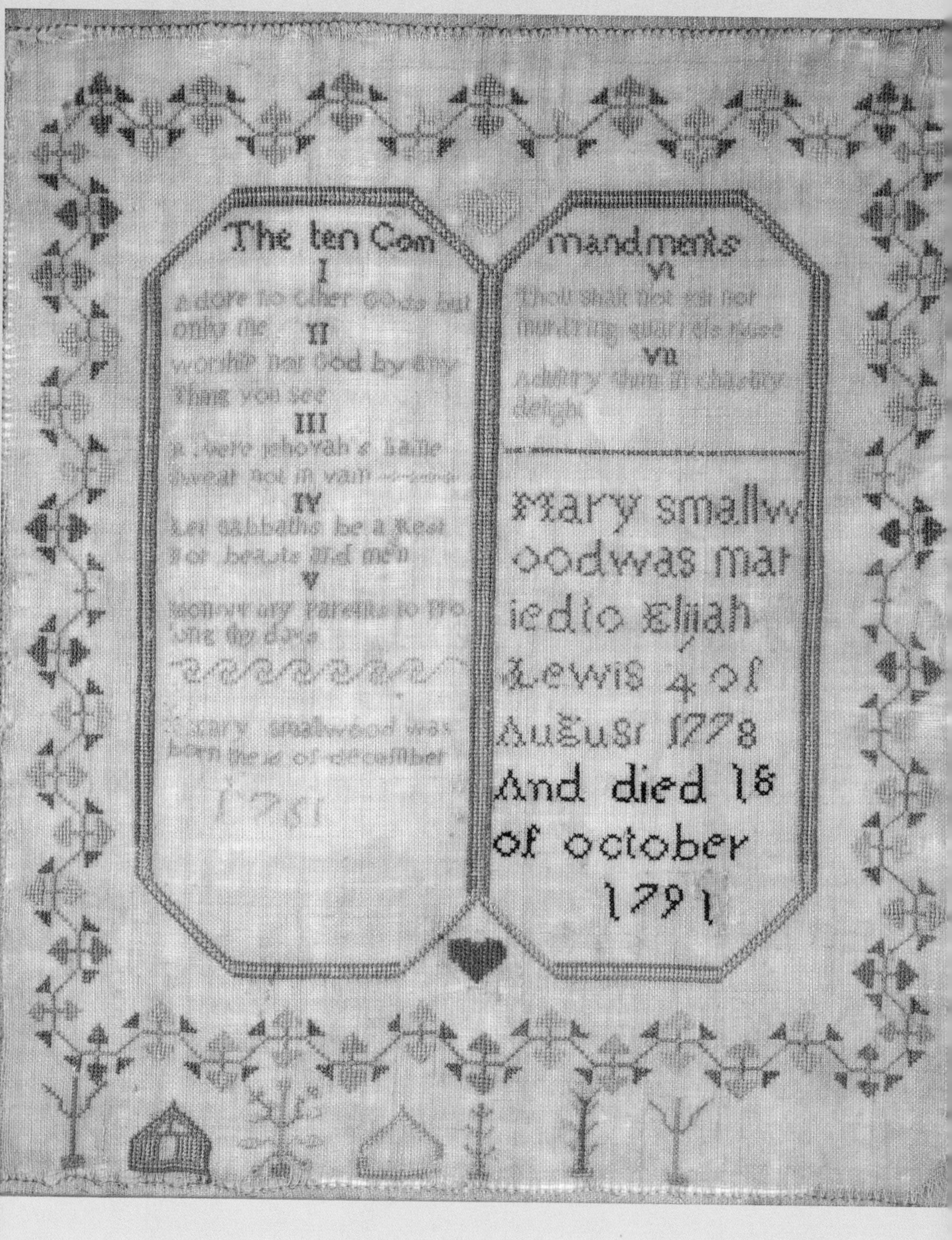

The ten Commandments

I

Adore no other Gods but only me

II

Worship not God by any thing you see

III

Revere Jehovah's name swear not in vain

IV

Let sabbaths be a Rest for beasts and men

V

Honour thy parents to prolong thy days

Mary smallwood was born the 15 of december 1761

VI

Thou shalt not kill nor murdring quarrels raise

VII

Adultery shun in chastity delight

mary smallwoodwas mar iedto Elijah Lewis 4 of Augusr 1778 And died 18 of october 1791

No. 03

Mary SMALLWOOD

A significant and poignant example of needlework produced in colonial America, Mary Smallwood's sampler is one of a few surviving Ten Commandments, or tablet, samplers made in the South (for an earlier Georgia example, worked by Sarah Jones, see catalogue number 2). Through its silk stitches—made by two women: one identified, the other unknown—we are able to reconstruct an otherwise sparsely documented life and reveal the remarkable story of a Georgia community's piety, prosperity, patriotism, and resilience.

Mary began her embroidery probably between the ages of six and twelve, but for unknown reasons never completed the sampler. She recorded her birth—"Mary Smallwood was born the [?] of December 1761"—but an unidentified hand added, in blue thread, the acknowledgment of her marriage: "Mary Smallwood was married to Elijah Lewis 4 of August 1778." This was followed with the solemn obituary in black thread: "and died 18 of October 1791." Taken in total, these three statements are nearly all that remain to document Mary's thirty years.

Central to the life of the Smallwood family and their community was Midway Congregational Church. The town of Midway, settled in 1752 and located in what is today Liberty County, south of Savannah, resembled many Georgia low country settlements, having an agricultural economy based on rice and slavery.[1] But the town is unique in the history of colonial Georgia because its community of fervent patriots was governed by New England's Puritan values.

Embroidered tablet-style sampler by Mary Smallwood (1761–1791) with later stitching by an unidentified hand, ca. 1770, 1778, and 1791. Worker's residence: Midway, Liberty County. Two-ply twisted silk thread on balanced plain weave linen. Stitches: counted cross over 2 x 2 threads, edges turned under twice and hemstitched. 15 5/8 x 13 1/2 inches (framed). Museum of Early Southern Decorative Arts. Acc. no. 5504

Apart from her sampler, the records of Midway Congregational Church provide some of the only documentation for Mary Smallwood's life.[2] The church recorded that Mary was baptized on January 10, 1762, and that her parents were Matthew Smallwood (d. 1772) and Rebecca Sumner (ca. 1740–bef. 1779).[3] Mary could claim a lineage among the earliest in America. Her Puritan ancestor Henry Way (1583–1667), from Dorset, England, sailed with his family in 1630 aboard the *Mary and John* and was an original settler of Dorchester, Massachusetts.[4] By 1695, members of the Way and Sumner families, along with other New England Puritans, had decided to relocate to a new settlement seventeen miles outside of Charleston, South Carolina, which they named, appropriately, Dorchester.[5]

While staying true to their New England principles and ideals, the Puritans of South Carolina's Dorchester community acclimated to the economic and cultural environment of the South. They became prosperous planters by growing rice in the swampy land along the Ashley River and Dorchester Creek. By 1725, more than 75 percent of the families residing in Dorchester owned slaves.[6] Twenty-five years later, in 1750, it became apparent to the congregation that Dorchester's land holdings had become too small for expanding commercial rice production further and for the subsequent dividing of lands among the community's children.[7] Nearby in the South Carolina low country, lands were not available for expansion, so they began to look elsewhere.

In 1751, the Trustees for the colony of Georgia remitted their ban on slavery, making suitable fertile acreage available for the cultivation of rice, which, at the time, required an enslaved labor force to grow and harvest profitably.[8] The Dorchester Puritans quickly applied for land grants totaling more than thirty thousand acres in St. John's Parish.[9] Echoing their earlier move from New England to South Carolina, this small, united congregation, including the Way and Sumner families, relocated their community to Midway, Georgia, between

1752 and 1756.[10] Among the original settlers of Midway were members of the Smallwood family and a young Rebecca Sumner.[11] Mary's grandmother, the widow Mary Bateman (d. 1772), had requested and received a land grant from the council of the royal government of Georgia in 1756. She immediately gave it in a "deed of love" to her son Matthew Smallwood.[12] In 1760, Matthew married Rebecca Sumner.[13] Their only surviving child was Mary.

Education among Midway's Congregationalists was an important concern. True to the example of New England's Puritan axom that education gave direction to piety, it is not surprising that Mary's sampler represents a religious theme. Ten Commandments samplers were depictions of the tablets that Moses delivered to the Israelites as described in the book of Exodus. Usually worked by young girls with Anglican backgrounds, the roots of tablet samplers can be traced back to England. Plaques or tablets displaying the Ten Commandments were important architectural features of early Anglican churches. The tablets were often situated behind the altarpiece and commonly incorporated the Lord's Prayer and Apostles' Creed for ornamentation and to encourage contemplation and reverence among the parishioners.[14]

Mary chose a poetic verse of the Ten Commandments written by the Rev. Thomas Dyche instead of Old Testament scripture; this same version appears on the sampler worked by Sarah Jones (catalogue number 2).

The poem, however, ends prematurely. It should have concluded with:

> Thou shalt not steal nor take another's right
> In bearing witness never tell a lie
> Covet not what may others damnify

Comparison of the two samplers results in a number of questions. Surrounding Sarah's sampler is the same patterned border as seen on Mary's, and there are other similarities between the two samplers. But what is the connection between the two girls and their samplers? Did they share family ties? Were they taught by the same person? Or did their teachers receive a common training? Ongoing research aims to find potential stylistic and cultural connections, establish common ground between the Smallwood and Jones families, and possibly identify the teachers of Mary Smallwood and Sarah Jones.

The incomplete nature of Mary's tablet sampler also raises questions about her life as a young woman. Was her education cut short? Did the deaths of her father and grandmother, in 1772, contribute to the abrupt end of her work? While the answers to these questions are unknown, through her sampler we do know the next chapter of Mary's life: her marriage to Captain Elijah Lewis (d. 1809) in 1778. And we know through the context of history that the Lewises' marriage began during a turbulent time, with war literally on their doorstep.

The British had a keen interest in the Midway settlement because of the community's Whig leanings. Two of the three men who signed the Declaration of Independence for Georgia—Button Gwinnett (1735–1777) and Dr. Lyman Hall (1724–1790)—attended the Midway Church.[15] The Battle of Midway Church was fought just a few months after Mary and Elijah's marriage. On November 27, 1778, the British burned the church, and residents in the area were forced from their homes. Many houses were destroyed, and valuable land was laid waste. Mary Smallwood's brother-in-law, Judah Lewis (d. 1778), was killed in the battle.[16]

The community rebounded after the American Revolution. Homes were rebuilt and land was replanted. The church building that stands today was constructed in 1792.[17] Mary and her husband returned to Midway, and Elijah served as the leader of a local militia, organizing and commanding a group of citizens to defend and respond to nearby raids by Creek Indians.[18]

Mary Smallwood's story concludes with black thread on her sampler: "and died 18 of October 1791." Church records confirm that date.[19] There is no evidence that Mary and Elijah had any surviving children, and it is unknown who completed the account of Mary's life in silk thread. Mary's sampler, however, is testament to a young woman who lived in a remarkable Georgia community amid momentous times.

Jenny Garwood

NOTES

1. Charles C. Jones Jr., *The Dead Towns of Georgia* (Savannah, GA: Morning News Steam Printing House, 1878), 150.
2. James Stacy, *History and Published Records of the Midway Congregational Church, Liberty County, Georgia* (1979; repr., Spartanburg, SC: Reprint Company, 2002).
3. Ibid., 112.
4. Ann Natalie Hansen, *The Dorchester Group: Puritanism and Revolution* (Columbus, OH: At the Sign of the Cock, 1987), 100; and Charles Edward Banks, *Planters of the Commonwealth: A Study of the Emigrants and Emigration in Colonial Times* (Boston: Riverside Press / Houghton Mifflin, 1930), 91.
5. George A. Rogers and R. Frank Saunders, *Swamp Water and Wiregrass: Historical Sketches of Coastal Georgia* (Macon, GA: Mercer University Press, 1984), 10.
6. Ibid., 18.
7. Hansen, 102–3.
8. *New Georgia Encyclopedia*, s.v. "Slavery in Colonial Georgia," by Betty Wood, www.georgiaencyclopedia.org/articles/history-archaeology/slavery-colonial-georgia. For a discussion on rice cultivation and use of enslaved labor, see Walter B. Edgar, *South Carolina; A History* (Columbia: University of South Carolina Press, 1998), 139–44.
9. Stacy, 17–18.
10. Rogers and Saunders, 19.
11. Stacy, 19.
12. Marion R. Hemperley, comp., *English Crown Grants in St. John Parish in Georgia, 1755–1775* (Atlanta: State Printing Office, 1972), 17.
13. Stacy, 75.
14. Louis P. Nelson, *The Beauty of Holiness: Anglicanism and Architecture in Colonial South Carolina* (Chapel Hill: University of North Carolina Press, 2008), 162–63.
15. Stacy, 86–88; and George Gillman Smith, DD, *The Story of Georgia and the Georgia People, 1732–1860: Complete in One Volume* (Macon, GA: privately printed, 1900), 48.
16. Stacy, 91.
17. Ibid., 226.
18. Jones, 28.
19. Stacy, 140.

No. 04

Mary CARR

See [how] the
[lilies] flourish
[white] and [fair]
see [how] the
[ravens] fed [from]
H[e]aven [are] then
[never] distrust
[thy] God [for] cloth
[and] Bread [while]
Lilies [flourish] and
[the] Ravens [fed]

Mary Carr Her
Sampler ended
the II July 1773

Before the advent of the American Revolution, an estimated third of Georgia's wealth was centered south of Savannah in St. John's Parish, one of three parishes that in 1777 would make up Liberty County.[1] In the 1750s, settlers established two towns: Midway and Sunbury. Midway (often spelled Medway in early documents), which boasted the area's first house of

Embroidered sampler worked by Mary Carr (1759–before 1811), dated July 11, 1773. Worker's residence: Sunbury, St. John's Parish. Two-ply twisted silk thread on balanced plain weave linen. Stitches: counted cross over 2 x 2 threads. 30 x 15 inches (framed). Midway Museum, Midway, Georgia

worship, Midway Congregational Church, had a mixed economy of rice production, lumber and naval stores, and a trade in deerskins with indigenous people (for a discussion of Midway, see catalogue number 3). The area's commercial center was the larger, port town of Sunbury, located on the Medway River, a tidal waterway that empties into St. Catherine's Sound and then to the Atlantic Ocean.

Mark Carr (d. 1767), Mary's paternal grandfather, had owned the tract upon which Sunbury was built. A member of Britain's Royal Scots Greys, he sailed to Georgia in 1738 as an officer in James Edward Oglethorpe's regiment. In 1748, Carr was granted five hundred acres along the Medway River. In 1758, he conveyed in trust three hundred acres in his possession for a town site, with an additional one hundred acres to be used as a town common.[2] Carr appointed five men as commissioners to sell the 496 lots he had laid out. The blueprint was similar to the plan of Savannah: a repeated pattern of connected neighborhoods and through streets organized around squares.[3] Sunbury would have three squares: King, Meeting, and Church.

A bird's eye view of Sunbury in 1773, the year Mary Carr completed her sampler, would have

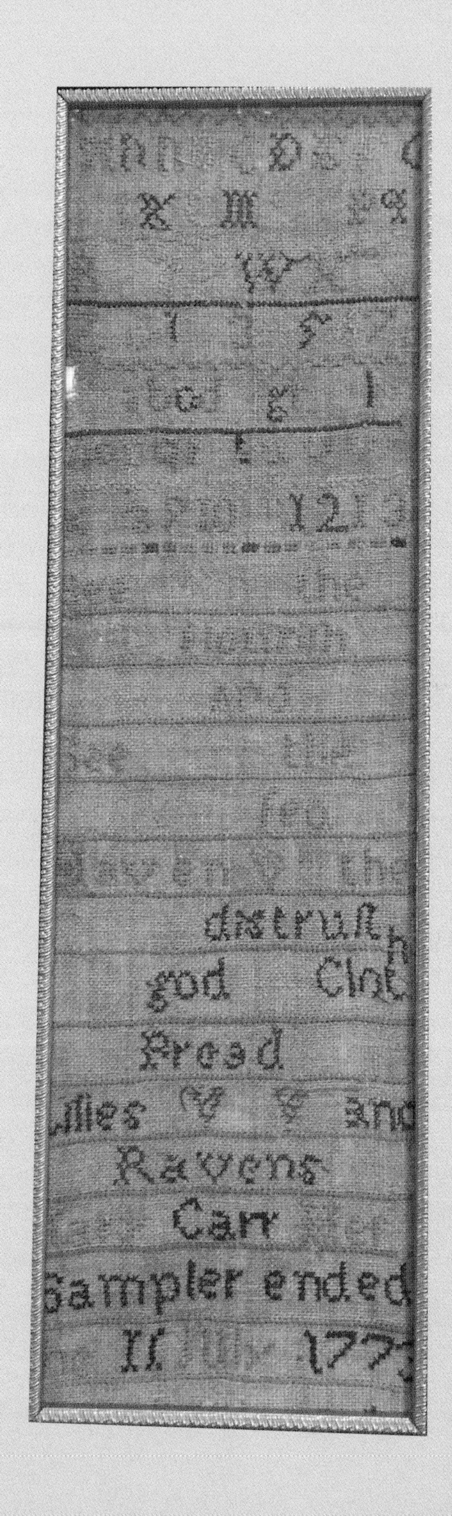

shown about a hundred homes "neatly built of wood framed, having pleasant Piasas [i.e., piazzas] round them."[4] Commercial buildings included shops, warehouses, and a customs house and naval office. Two roads led from the town. Sunbury's five wharves were equipped to accommodate multiple square-rigged vessels at the same time.[5] William Bartram noted of his visit to the town a year later, in April 1774, "The inhabitants are genteel & wealthy, either Merchants, or Planters from the Country who resort here in the Summer & Autum, to pertake of the Salubrious Sea breese, Bathing & sporting on the Sea Islands."[6]

The lettering is now much worn; the majority of the inscription is lacking or difficult to decipher . . .

Mary was about fourteen when she embroidered alphabets, numbers, a verse, and a personal inscription on a long and quite narrow scrap of linen. The lettering is now much worn; the majority of the inscription is lacking or difficult to decipher (in the above transcription, missing words and letters are in brackets). "See how the lilies flourish white and fair" is the first line of a four-line verse popular among eighteenth-century sampler makers in England as well as colonial America, as evinced by the number of online entries listed in a Google search of the poem. The poem also was stitched by two of South Carolina's low country girls: Elizabeth Hext in 1743 and Martha Motte in 1751.[7]

The verse was originally published in Rev. Thomas Dyche's *A Guide to the English Tongue in Two Parts,* a primer intended for the education of boys. The lines are part of a series of twenty four-line rhymes that Dyche composed for students to copy as writing practice.[8] The *Guide* offered the correct pronunciation and spelling of the English language of its time as well as prescriptions in virtuous living. As a schoolmaster teaching in London when this book saw its first publication, in 1709, Dyche keenly perceived the potential influence of his work. Those who applied his standards for speaking and writing would, through practice, cultivate the standards of learned men, who practiced gentility and civility:

> These Rules are well design'd, to take away
> The Scandal that upon our Nation lay;
> Where Elegance a Stranger was, and few
> The Beauties of their Mother-Language knew.
> These Rules must rectify both Tongue and Pen,
> If Youth wou'd speak and write like learned Men.[9]

In promoting taste as well as morals, Dyche's work had unintended results: while boys practiced with ink and pen, girls practiced with needle and thread.

Although Mark Carr has received much attention in the histories of Georgia, mentions of his children and grandchildren—including Mary—are more difficult to find in the primary sources. Accompanying Carr on the voyage in 1738 were his three children: Judith, William, and Thomas. Their mother, Jane Perkins Carr, did not emigrate. In Georgia, Carr had a relationship with an Elizabeth Rutherford, which produced another daughter, Elizabeth.[10]

Little is known about Mary's father, William (b. ca. 1732); in 1752 he was granted five hundred acres on the Newport River, south of the site of Sunbury.[11] Mary was the first of two daughters born to him and Grace Hastings Carr in the Sunbury District in 1759. She was baptized at the Midway Congregational Church in July of that year, but her family may have been Anglican. Although the Church of England was established as Georgia's official religion in 1758 (in Sunbury, the Anglican church was located in Church Square), most of the permanent residents of St. John's Parish were Congregationalists and attended Sunday services at the Midway church. By 1767, Midway had engaged a second minister for the congregation's residents. The area's Anglicans had difficulty, however, retaining a minister: "those who Profess the established Religion of the Church of England are not sufficient to maintain a Clergyman."[12] Midway's minister accommodated local members of the Church of England by performing baptisms and weddings when necessary.[13]

Mary lost her father at least a year before she began her marking sampler. In April of 1772, Grace Carr was a widow with "two Children and three Negroes" when she petitioned the colony's executive council for her own "Land for Cultivation" in St. John's Parish—specifically, one hundred acres adjoining the land of her deceased husband.[14] When Mary wed Henry Myers in 1784, the ceremony was not performed at Midway. Over time, the Myerses owned and sold a number of lots in Sunbury, but it is unclear whether Mary inherited these properties from her father or if the couple jointly acquired them.[15] The last of the land transactions took place in 1802; Mary's death likely occurred in the next decade.

NOTES

1. The other two were the parishes of St. James and St. Andrew.
2. The conveyance is transcribed in John McKay Sheftall, *Sunbury on the Medway* (Atlanta: State of Georgia, Department of Natural Resources, Office of Planning and Research, Historic Preservation Section, 1977), 6–8.
3. A copy of an early plat of the town is reproduced in Sheftall, 111, illustration 11.
4. William Bartram, "Travels in Georgia and Florida, 1773–74: A Report to Dr. John Fothergill," ed. Francis Harper, *Transactions of the American Philosophical Society*, ns, vol. 33, part 2 (November 1943): 134.
5. Hugh McCall, *The History of Georgia* (1811; repr., Atlanta: A. B. Caldwell, 1909), 177.
6. Bartram, 134.

7. Elizabeth Hext's sampler is in the Charleston Museum, and Martha Motte's sampler is in a private collection. The former is illustrated in Jan Hiester and Kathleen Staples, *This Have I Done: Samplers and Embroideries from Charleston and the Lowcountry* (Greenville, SC: Curious Works Press; Charleston: Charleston Museum), 16. The latter is illustrated in Lynn C. Tinley, "Learning and Godliness Cultivated Together: Early Eighteenth-Century Samplers from Boston, Philadelphia, and the South Carolina Low Country" (PhD diss., Emory University, 2012), figure 39.
8. Thomas Dyche, *A Guide to the English Tongue in Two Parts*, 2nd ed. (London, 1710), 127–29.
9. Address to Thomas Dyche, "my Ingenious Friend," by Nahum Tate, poet laureate. Ibid., n.p.
10. Mark Carr, will dated December 4, 1767, Will Books, Colony of Georgia, RG 49-1-5, Georgia Archives. The four children are named in his will.
11. Allen D. Candler, comp., *Colonial Records of the State of Georgia*, vol. 6 (Atlanta: Franklin-Turner, 1907), 370–72.
12. Petition, dated July 2, 1771, Records of the Society for the Propagation of the Gospel in Foreign Parts, quoted in Sheftall, 17.
13. For example, in 1764, the Anglican minister, Rev. John Alexander, was married to Hannah Godfrey at Midway Congregational Church.
14. Candler, 291.
15. Sheftall, 185–212.

No. 05

Mary Anna STEVENS

Throughout the antebellum period the Midway people were justly known for their remarkable way of life. No planting community could boast deeper religious convictions, higher intellectual cultivation, gentler social refinement, or greater material wealth.

—Robert Manson Myers, *The Children of Pride*[1]

Mary Anna Stevens was born into one of the well-to-do planter families of coastal Liberty County. Her father, John Stevens (1777–1832), was master of Palmyra Plantation and named after his father, John Stevens (1737–1777), a member of Georgia's provincial congress. Her mother, Amarintha Munro Stevens (1785–1859), was the daughter of Savannah and Sunbury merchant and Loyalist Simon Munro.[2] Palmyra, Mary Anna's birthplace, was situated southwest of the port town of Sunbury, along the marshy area created by the North Newport and Medway rivers and across from Colonel's Island. The area was well suited to the production not only of rice but also of sea island cotton, a high-quality but low-yield plant that requires intensive care during the entire crop cycle, from planting through harvest.[3]

By the time of Mary Anna's birth, in 1817, Liberty County had survived two wars (the British had occupied Sunbury in the Revolutionary War but remained off the coast during the War of 1812) and the destructive and deadly Antigua-Charleston hurricane of September 1804. In 1797, the county

---

Embroidered sampler worked by Mary Anna Stevens (1817–1885), dated April 12, 1827. Worker's residence: Palmyra Plantation, Liberty County. Two-ply twisted silk thread on balanced plain weave linen. Stitches: counted cross over 2 x 2 threads; square eyelet over 4 x 4 threads; counted satin. 19 x 16 1/2 inches (framed). Midway Museum, Midway, Georgia

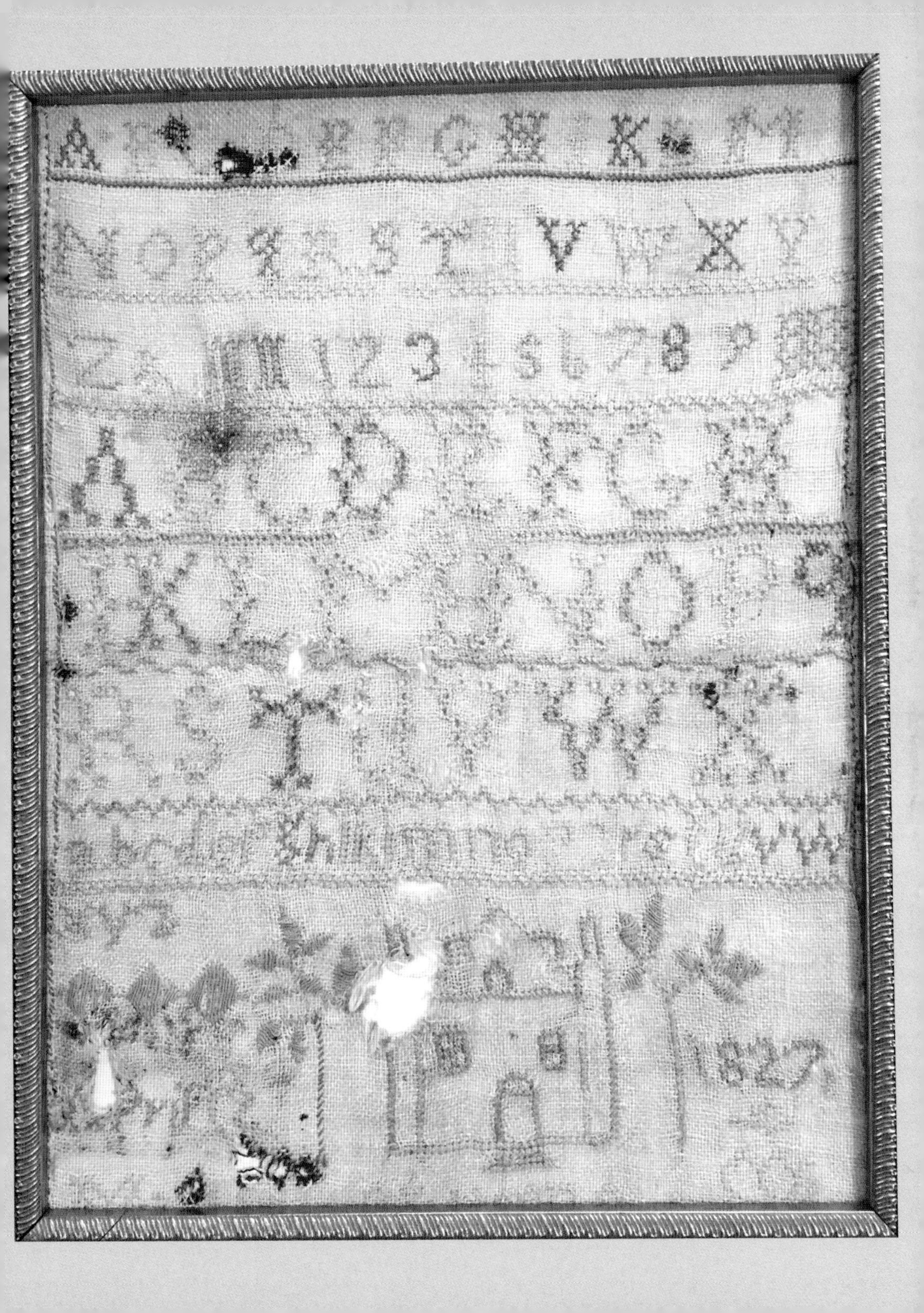
1827

seat had moved from Sunbury to Riceborough, a port town on the North Newport River, about eight miles inland. This shift marked the beginning of Sunbury's gradual decline as a thriving community.[4]

In 1820, the Stevens family included eight children. At that time John Stevens owned sixty-three slaves. Those who were old enough—at least forty souls—worked the fields; tended to household, kitchen, and yard duties; or worked at textile tasks. Amarintha Stevens would have supervised all but the fields, perhaps assisted by Mary's older sisters, Caroline Georgia (1806–1824) and Harriet Elizabeth (1811–1887).

To protect valuable property, continue farming, and avoid attacks by Union troops, many of Georgia's coastal families made the decision to move households and slaves inland.

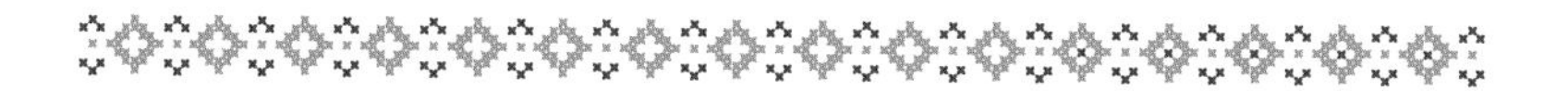

In addition to the "hospitable bearing" and "delicate and refined deportment" she was expected to acquire by observing the examples of her mother and other female relatives and friends, Mary Anna, like other young ladies in the wider neighborhood, was exposed to an academic education appropriate for her sex.[5] She may have attended classes at nearby Sunbury Academy for reading, writing, English grammar, history, and mathematics. Her father was secretary of the school's trustees in the 1810s and 1820s. This institution was known to accept female students; however, there is no evidence that needlework was part of the curriculum. Thus, her needlework education may have mirrored that of one of the daughters in the extended family of her neighbor, Rev. Charles Colcock Jones (1804–1863). Jones, who owned Maybank Plantation on Colonel's Island, just across the marsh from Palmyra, engaged private tutors for his sons and daughters. One of Jones's relatives sent a daughter to a fashionable ladies' seminary in Philadelphia; another relation attended a boarding school in Charleston.[6]

In about 1837, Mary Anna wed Oliver Winn Stevens (1812–1882; no blood relation) and settled in Liberty County. Oliver planted cotton using enslaved labor and conducted a school, which in 1840 had twelve scholars. Between 1838 and 1858, nine children were born to the couple. Like her girlhood neighbor Mary Jones, wife of Rev. Jones, whom the couple saw from time to time, Mary Anna likely devoted part of her daily activities to domestic duties: "cutting out, planning, fitting, or sewing, giving attention to the clothing department and to the condition of the furniture of chambers, curtains, towels, linens, etc."[7]

"We are having moving times in old Liberty," wrote Rev. Jones to his stepdaughter Eliza Robarts in 1862, "the occurrences of the first revolution coming round in the second."[8] To protect valuable property, continue farming, and avoid attacks by Union troops, many of Georgia's coastal families made the decision to move households and slaves inland. Oliver Stevens's name was among those Jones enumerated in his letter as neighbors intending to relocate. The Stevens family left Liberty County sometime between 1862 and 1863, resettling permanently in Quitman, the seat of Brooks County. According to census records, Oliver was still teaching in 1880. The circumstances of Mary Anna's last years are unknown.

NOTES

1. Robert Manson Myers, *Children of Pride: A True Story of Georgia and the Civil War* (New Haven, CT: Yale University Press, 1972), 10.

2. Public Records Office (PRO), Audit Office, class 13, volume 26, folios 785–86. Munro was banished from Georgia because of his Tory position and did not return permanently until 1787. His sometime partners were Roger Kelsall and Andrew Darling. In 1764 and 1765, they trafficked in European and East India goods, rum, wine, salt, and African slaves. See, for example, *Georgia Gazette*, March 29, 1764, and May 23, 1765.
3. For an in-depth discussion of the origins of sea island cotton, see S. G. Stephens, "The Origin of Sea Island Cotton," *Agricultural History* 50, no. 2 (April 1976): 391–99.
4. For a discussion of colonial Sunbury, see catalogue no. 4.
5. Charles C. Jones Jr. to Rev. and Mrs. C. C. Jones, July 4, 1854, in Myers, 51. Liberty County resident Charles C. Jones Jr. used these and other solicitous phrases to describe the manners of friends from Georgia who were staying at a hotel in New Haven, Connecticut, whom he visited there. Their bearing, he said, brought to mind "the attractions of a Southern home—in striking contrast . . . to the 'belongings' of a Northern residence."
6. Myers, 20–22.
7. Rev. Charles C. Jones to Charles C. Jones Jr., May 22, 1854, ibid., 35.
8. Rev. Charles C. Jones to Eliza Robarts, December 13, 1862, ibid., 998.

No. 06

Frances ROE

Self Goverment
May I govern My passions
with absolute Sway
And grow wiser and better
as Life weres Away

rances Roe's puzzling inscription "this work Ended in Savannah" is the first clue to unraveling her family's complex migration story. She possibly began her embroidery sometime in Baltimore in 1815 and completed it in Savannah the following year.

Born in New York in about 1758, Conrad "Rouw" was making biscuits in Philadelphia by 1785. On July 14 of that year, he married Mary Chamberlain at the First Reformed (German Reformed) Church of Philadelphia.[1] The couple remained in the city for a few years, but resettled in Abington, Harford County, Maryland, by 1800 and now had two young sons (Samuel and Charles) and three daughters (Maria, Hester, and Eliza).[2]

Rouw moved the family a second time, from Abington to Baltimore, in 1810. The federal census for that year indicates that two more daughters had been born: Sarah and sampler maker Frances (the couple's last child, Amelia, was born shortly after the census was taken). In August of 1813, Rouw, now listed as Conrad "Rowe," joined the thousands of citizens who had committed to the defense of Maryland during the War of 1812, serving as a private in the 39th Regiment of the state's militia.[3] The family was still

Self Goverment
May I govern My paſ sions
with absolute Sway
And grow wiser and better
as Life wears Away .
Frances Roe was
Born Decemberth 7 in
the year of our Lord
. 1803 . this work
Ended in Savannah .

in Baltimore in 1814, and a city directory indicates that Rowe was working as a distiller.[4]

According to historical records, here Conrad "Roe" worked as both a baker and distiller, and here Frances "ended" her sampler, perhaps under the guidance of her mother or one of the city's many schoolmistresses.

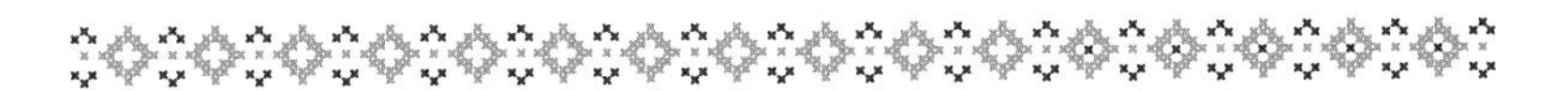

The war years meant bankruptcy for many of Baltimore's most successful merchant families; 1815 brought peace, but the city had few exports for overseas buyers. Perhaps this economic downturn prompted Rowe to uproot his family for a third time. In 1815 or early 1816, they moved to Savannah, to a section of the city known then as Spring Hill. According to historical records, here Conrad "Roe" worked as both a baker and distiller, and here Frances "ended" her sampler, perhaps under the guidance of her mother or one of the city's many schoolmistresses.[5] Although there is no proof that Frances started her embroidery in Baltimore, there is a favorable comparison between her rendering of a Federal-style house, flanked by trees, and the stitched houses worked by Baltimore girls in the 1810s.[6] Frances's verse, "Self Government," is an adaptation of two lines of the chorus of a twenty-verse poem, "The Wish," written by the English astronomer and poet Walter Pope (1628–1714) and published in 1697.[7] By the nineteenth century, these lines were quoted in published Sunday school lessons and Christian devotionals on both sides of the Atlantic.

Although Frances's brothers, Samuel and Charles, made names for themselves in Savannah, nothing further is known of her life. Between September and

---

Embroidered sampler by Frances Roe (b. 1803), ca. 1816. Worked in Savannah, Chatham County. Two-ply twisted silk thread on balanced plain weave linen. Stitches: counted cross over 1 x 1 and 2 x 2 threads; surface satin. 17 5/8 x 16 3/4 inches (framed). Georgia Museum of Art, University of Georgia; Museum purchase with funds provided by Alex and Claire Crumbley and the Chaparral Foundation, Linda and David Chesnut, and Robert and Suzanne Currey. GMOA 2014.50

October of 1816, Savannah experienced an epidemic of yellow and bilious fevers.[8] Conrad was diagnosed with the latter and died in Spring Hill on September 3. Frances's mother, Mary, died of an unspecified fever a year later, on October 10, 1817.[9]

NOTES

1. "Pennsylvania Marriage Licenses, 1784–86," in *Pennsylvania Archives*, Sixth Series, vol. 6, ed. Thomas Lynch Montgomery (Harrisburg, PA: Harrisburg Publishing, 1907), 305. The license bond includes Rouw's occupation. The spelling of Conrad's surname changes in legal documents as he and his family move from Philadelphia to Abington and then to Baltimore, and finally to Savannah: Rouw, Rowe, and Roe.
2. Conrad Rowe, 1800 United States Federal Census, Harford, Maryland, District 1; Ancestry.com.
3. Index to Compiled Service Records of Volunteer Soldiers Who Served during the War of 1812, National Archives and Records Administration (NARA), record group 94, Fold3.com.
4. James Lakin, *The Baltimore Directory and Register for 1814–15* (Baltimore: J. C. O'Reilly, 1814), 166.
5. Conrad's profession and place of birth were recorded in Savannah, Georgia, Vital Records, 1803–1966; Ancestry.com.
6. See, for example, houses in the "eyeglass gate" group in Gloria Seaman Allen, "Baltimore Town and Country," in *A Maryland Sampling: Girlhood Embroidery, 1738–1860* (Baltimore: Maryland Historical Society, 2007), 195–234.
7. In 1785, Benjamin Franklin wrote of his long-held fondness for Pope's chorus, which he called "The Old Man's Wish" and which he sang. See Mark Skousen, ed., *The Completed Autobiography by Benjamin Franklin*, vol. 2, *1757–1790* (Washington, DC: Regnery Publishing, 2007), 388–89.
8. *Memoirs of Georgia*, vol. 2 (Atlanta: Southern Historical Association, 1895), 107.
9. Conrad and Mary Roe's deaths were recorded in Savannah, Georgia, Vital Records, 1803–1966; Ancestry.com.

Letitia Malvina MILLS

Letitia Malvina Mills (ca. 1820–1850) worked an impressive sampler, all the more remarkable given that she was six years old when she completed her stitching ("in her 7th Year" means she was six).[1] The central panel of her embroidery is notable for its two-story house with raised basement, baroque roofline, and tall chimneys, flanked by tall, narrow trees. Birds are in abundance, including a peacock with a trio of tail feathers. Some of these motifs resemble forms found on samplers made in the South Carolina low country during roughly the same time period.[2] While not conclusive, these similarities hint at the possibility of Letitia's instructor having come from the Charleston area.[3]

Born in about 1820, Letitia Malvina Mills was a city girl. Her father, William C. Mills (d. ca. 1848), owned a quarter lot with a house on-site in Anson Ward, the area surrounding Savannah's Oglethorpe Square.[4] Before 1827, he had acquired an additional lot and house on Williams Street, all of which he signed over to his wife, Sarah S. Lewis Mills (d. ca. 1857), by that year.[5] In 1818 and 1819, William had been involved as a plaintiff and defendant in two separate lawsuits.[6] Although successful in both actions, he perhaps wished to protect his property in any future litigation by transferring ownership to Sarah.

In 1842, at Savannah's Trinity Methodist Church, Letitia married Lewis Tattnall Turner, a physician. The ceremony was officiated by the widely respected Rev. James Ezekiel Evans.[7] The couple returned to Turner's home in the hamlet of Hardwick, in Bryan County, southeast of Savannah.

ABCD

UWXY

Letitia Malvina Mills her work ended August
29 in her 7 Year Savannah

Between 1842 and 1850, Letitia bore four children. She died unexpectedly in Hardwick after a short illness, on February 22, 1850, and merited obituaries in two Savannah newspapers. In reading them, one has the sense that her married life in Hardwick was not as stimulating as her Savannah childhood and that she actively created and maintained friendships in the city. Stressing her affability, one eulogy draws attention to these long-distance relationships—"her sudden death has cast a gloom over her friends who, but a week ago, enjoyed her society in this city."[8] The other, more positive, evokes the warm ties of kinship and community she must have experienced throughout her life: "The very many endearing qualities of the deceased in the character of wife, mother, sister, daughter and friend, render eulogy unnecessary to perpetuate her fame."[9]

Letitia's sampler descended in her family. Curator Kimberly Ivey notes that an extensive newspaper account of a family wedding held in 1933 describes Letitia's sampler and records that it was a wedding gift.[10]

NOTES

1. I thank Kimberly Ivey, curator of textiles and historic interiors, Colonial Williamsburg Foundation, for generously sharing her research on Letitia Mills and documentation of her sampler.
2. See, for example, the work of Easter Budd, Sarah Ann Wilcox, and Jane Eliza Taylor illustrated in Jan Hiester and Kathleen Staples, *This Have I Done: Samplers and Embroideries from Charleston and the Lowcountry* (Greenville, SC: Curious Works Press; Charleston, SC: Charleston Museum, 2001).
3. One candidate is the wife of a Mr. Phillips; in 1825, Phillips left his position at Rockville Academy, in the town of Rockville, Charleston County—north of Charleston—to establish a day school in Savannah. An advertisement in the *Georgian* (Savannah, GA) for July 4, 1826, announced that Mrs. Phillips would instruct young ladies in needlework and marking (i.e., sampler making). The couple's academy flourished until at least the end of 1829.
4. In 1824, William was taxed on his improved real estate, in addition to two dogs, a gig, and four slaves. See William C. Mills, Tax Digest for 1824, Savannah, Georgia, Land Tax and Property Records, 1809–1838, Ancestry.com.
5. Sarah L. Mills by W. C. Mills, Tax Digest for 1827, Savannah, Georgia, Land Tax and Property Records, 1809–1838, Ancestry.com.
6. William C. Mills, Savannah, Georgia, Court Records, 1790–1934, Ancestry.com.

Embroidered sampler by Letitia Malvina Mills (ca. 1820–1850), dated August 29 (ca. 1826). Worker's residence: Savannah, Chatham County. Two-ply twisted silk thread on balanced plain weave linen (30 x 30 threads per inch). Stitches: counted cross over 1 x 1 and 2 x 2 threads; crossed corners (rice); square eyelet over 4 x 4 threads, counted satin. Not displayed in exhibition. Courtesy Colonial Williamsburg Foundation; Museum purchase. 2013-81

7. Through the Methodist Episcopal Church, Rev. Evans helped establish Emory College—now Emory University, in Atlanta—in 1836.
8. *Savannah (GA) Daily Morning News*, February 26, 1850.
9. *Savannah (GA) Daily Republican*, February 26, 1850. A little over a year after Letitia's death, Lewis married her sister, Sarah Screven Mills.
10. Museum label for Letitia Malvina Mills, DeWitt Wallace Decorative Arts Museum, Colonial Williamsburg Foundation, March 13, 2015.

Family member of COSMO RICHARDSONE

Tribute To The Memory
OF
Dr. Cosmo P. Richardsone.
By Henry R. Jackson.

Savannah mourns! And cannot stay
Her grief to lose so dear a head;
And sends her children forth to pay
The last, sad tribute to the dead!

No pageant train, no empty show,
No burial of the simply great;–
Such multitudes but yield to woe
When noble hearts have ceased to beat!

Friend of the friendless, poor, and weak!
Thou model of the good and brave!
Unnumbered tongues thy virtues speak,
Unnumbered hearts melt o'er thy grave!

A high and holy homage! meet
For burial such as thine alone,
More honored in thy winding sheet
Than monarch on his jewelled throne!

Since not too soon thy frame was chilled,
For thou had'st reached a shining goal,
And lived an earnest life, and filled
The measure of a perfect soul!

And left the world in debt to thee–
A debt it will not blush to own;–
A fame of rare sublimity,
A monument of true renown!

Go! generous spirit! purer skies
Receive thee with a warm embrace!
Tis here alone the shadow lies–
Since none can fill thy vacant place!

It is for us and not for thee,
Thou angel of resplendent wing!
The grave has had a victory,
And death a keen and poisoned sting!

Savannah, Feb. 8th, 1852

We regret to announce the death, in this city, at 1 o'clock this afternoon, of Dr. Cosmo P. Richardsone, in the 48th year of his age. Dr. R. was born in Edinburgh, Scotland, and came to Savannah when but three years old. He has resided here, we believe, ever since, and in the meantime, has amassed a handsome fortune, and established a reputation as a skillful physician and high-minded, honorable gentleman, enjoyed by but few men of his years. At the time of his death, he was a member of the Board of Aldermen and the commanding officer of the Savannah Volunteer Guards—the oldest infantry company in the city or State.

There are but few men in the city whose death would create so great a void as that of Dr. Richardsone. He was confessedly one of the first physicians in Savannah, and was in the possession of a large and lucrative practice. But high as he deservedly ranked as a physician, it was as a high-toned, chivalric gentleman, a ripe scholar, and an enterprising citizen, that he filled so large a space in the public estimation.

—*Savannah Republican*, February 6, 1852

At six feet tall, "with a high forehead, gray eyes, long nose, small mouth, with two scars on his chin, brown hair, fair complexion, and long face," Cosmo Politus Richardsone (1804–1852) was considered by some contemporaries to be the best doctor in Savannah.[1] He had studied medicine there and then at the Charleston Medical College in South Carolina, receiving a degree in 1828. His thesis was on yellow fever.[2] Over the years, his patients encompassed all racial and socioeconomic groups. For example, one of his early professional responsibilities was to the inmates at the Savannah Poor House and Hospital as one of their attending physicians.[3] Accepting only indigent whites, this institution treated ill and pregnant women, maimed sailors, ailing men, and orphaned children.[4] In September 1834, Richardsone was at the plantation of a Major Whiteman, located about ten miles from Savannah, to attend to a cholera outbreak there, likely among enslaved workers. At least fifteen people were infected; five had died within the first twenty-four hours of the outbreak.[5]

According to Savannah Health Department records, Richardsone died February 6, 1852, of a cancerous brain tumor.[6] It is likely that his widow

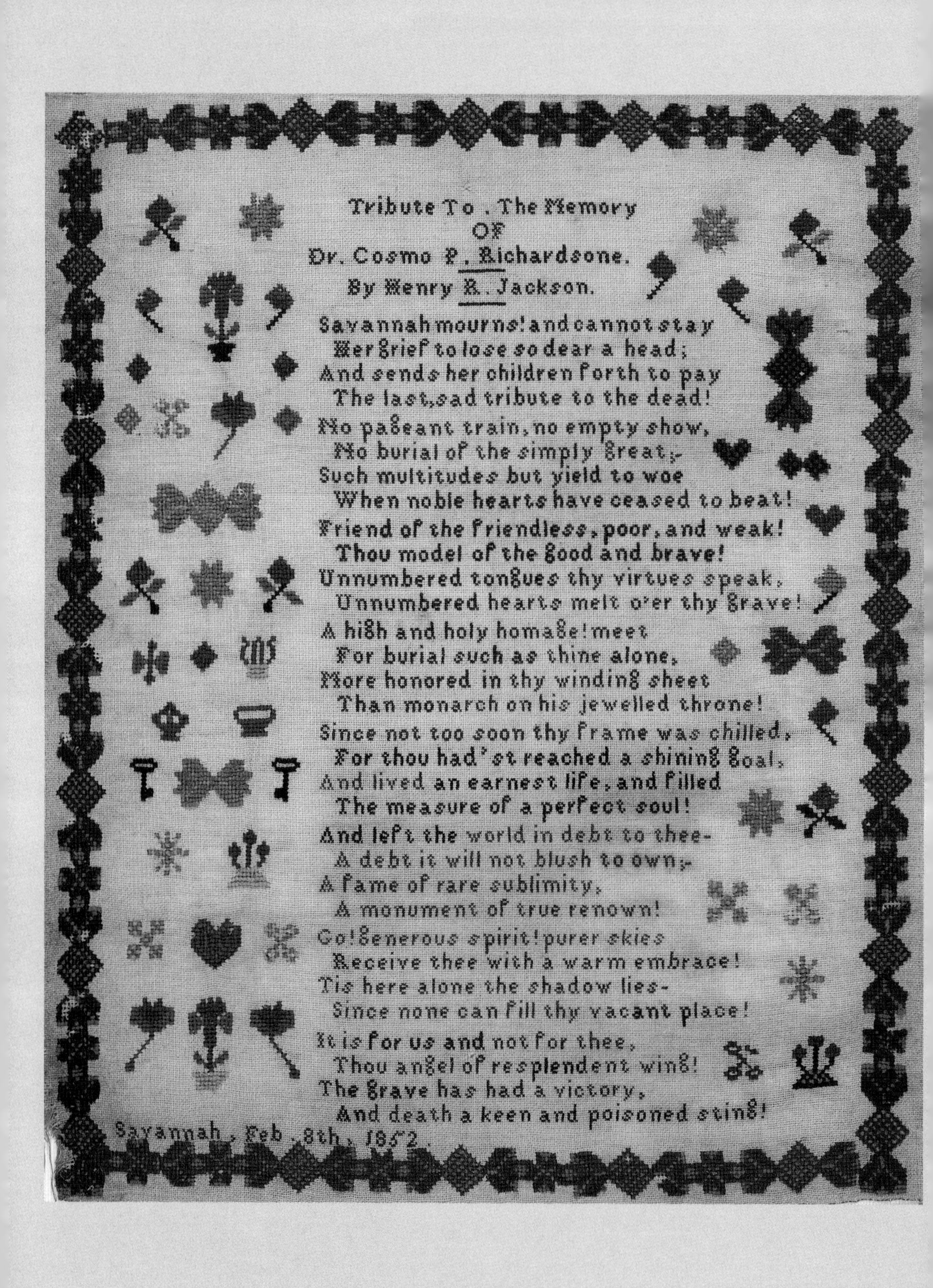
Tribute To . The Memory
OF
Dr. Cosmo P. Richardsone.
By Henry R. Jackson.
Savannah mourns! and cannot stay
Her grief to lose so dear a head;
And sends her children forth to pay
The last, sad tribute to the dead!
No pageant train, no empty show,
No burial of the simply great;-
Such multitudes but yield to woe
When noble hearts have ceased to beat!
Friend of the friendless, poor, and weak!
Thou model of the good and brave!
Unnumbered tongues thy virtues speak,
Unnumbered hearts melt o'er thy grave!
A high and holy homage! meet
For burial such as thine alone,
More honored in thy winding sheet
Than monarch on his jewelled throne!
Since not too soon thy frame was chilled,
For thou had'st reached a shining goal,
And lived an earnest life, and filled
The measure of a perfect soul!
And left the world in debt to thee-
A debt it will not blush to own;-
A fame of rare sublimity,
A monument of true renown!
Go! generous spirit! purer skies
Receive thee with a warm embrace!
Tis here alone the shadow lies-
Since none can fill thy vacant place!
It is for us and not for thee,
Thou angel of resplendent wing!
The grave has had a victory,
And death a keen and poisoned sting!
Savannah, Feb. 8th, 1852.

Elizabeth (ca. 1816–1890), perhaps with the help of daughter Margaret (ca. 1843–1898), embroidered this memorial. The scattered geometric and floral motifs were probably gleaned from the booklets of charted patterns published in Europe and widely distributed in the United States. The poem, dated the day of his funeral and never published, was the work of Henry Rootes Jackson (1820–1898), a lawyer, politician, and Confederate general. (Jackson was also a public speaker and a poet; his book *Tallulah and Other Poems* was published in 1850.) The heavy use of punctuation—dashes, semicolons, and exclamation marks—in the stitched version is unusual for embroidered sampler verses and emphasizes the care with which the maker copied what was likely Jackson's manuscript.

NOTES

1. Register of Passport Applications, 14 Nov 1834–08 May 1843, National Archives and Records Administration (NARA), Fold3.com.
2. *Georgian* (Savannah, GA), April 14, 1828.
3. See, for example, the announcement in the *Georgian* (Savannah, GA), October 7, 1828.
4. For a fuller discussion of the Poor House and Hospital, see Walter J. Fraser, *Savannah in the Old South* (Athens: University of Georgia Press, 2003), 280.
5. Reported in the *Macon (GA) Weekly Telegraph*, September 11, 1834.
6. Cosmo Richardson, Savannah, Georgia, Select Board of Health and Health Department Records, 1824–1864, Ancestry.com.

Embroidered memorial tribute to Cosmo P. Richardsone, attributed to a family member, ca. 1852. Worked in Savannah, Chatham County. Plied merino wool yarn on balanced plain weave linen; top and bottom edges are selvages; right and left edges turned under twice and hemmed. Stitches: counted cross over 1 x 1 and 2 x 2 threads. 18 3/4 x 15 1/8 inches. The Miller Collection

No. 09

Unidentified maker
SISTERS OF OUR LADY MERCY

Skillfully executed, this lively and detailed basket of roses with birds is the smallest example in a collection of canvaswork pictures made in the nineteenth century by unnamed sisters at the Convent of the Sisters of Our Lady of Mercy, in Savannah. The composition was created by following a printed and hand-colored chart called a Berlin work pattern. These paper patterns were developed in the first decade of the 1800s in Germany and produced for most of the century in Berlin and Vienna for European, British, and American distribution.[1]

Each Berlin work pattern is a printed point paper, similar to graph paper, the squares of which are marked with various symbols. Each square represents a cross or tent stitch; each symbol represents a different color (blank squares denote no stitch or a stitch executed in a background color). In the first half of the nineteenth century, artists colored the patterns by hand before they were sold, which made the patterns easier to read and facilitated the selection of yarn colors. According to the most popular early author of embroidery handbooks, London's Frances Lambert, "in some of these patterns there are considerably above half a million of small squares, like those of a mosaic, to be separately coloured."[2]

The Sisters of Our Lady of Mercy was founded in Charleston, South Carolina, in 1829 by four women from Baltimore, Maryland, who wished to

---

Embroidered picture by an unknown member of the Convent of the Sisters of Our Lady of Mercy, ca. 1860. Worked in Savannah, Chatham County. Plied wool yarn on balanced weave fabric. Stitches: counted cross over 2 x 2 threads. Frame dimensions: 29 1/4 x 28 1/4 inches. Collection of St. Vincent's Academy, Savannah, Georgia

live a vowed life. The women had met Bishop John England (1786–1842), Charleston's first Roman Catholic bishop, while he was attending the first provincial council for American bishops in Baltimore. They modeled this new religious community of women after the Sisters of Charity founded by Elizabeth Seton in Maryland and based its rule on that of St. Vincent of Paul—to offer assistance to individuals in need. In 1830, the sisters established a boarding and day school in Charleston, the Academy of Our Lady of Mercy, which offered basic academic subjects along with music, art, and embroidery.[3]

In June 1845, six members of the Charleston community arrived in Savannah to establish a branch house, led by Mother Mary Vincent Mahoney (d. 1873). Almost immediately, the sisters arranged to open both an orphanage and a school, the Academy of Saint Vincent of Paul (later St. Vincent's Academy). Among the expenditures for St. Vincent's Academy during its first five years of operation were payments for general "marketing"; beef, ham, potatoes, and bread; cow feed (the sisters likely ran a dairy on the property); mattresses; millinery goods and bonnets for the orphans; carpentry work; pipes for indoor running water and a bathtub; and needlework supplies.[4]

A Catholic almanac reported in 1853 that the convent had "eleven professed sisters, who observe the rule of St. Vincent of Paul. To it is attached a Boarding and Day School for young ladies, containing about 90 pupils, as also an Orphan Asylum for girls, which maintains at present 26 female orphans; and a free day school, which averages about 100 pupils."[5]

NOTES

1. For examples of Berlin work patterns and Berlin wool embroidery done in the United States, see Margaret Vincent, *The Ladies' Work Table: Domestic Needlework in Nineteenth-Century America* (Allentown, PA: Allentown Art Museum, 1988).
2. Frances Lambert, *The Hand-Book of Needlework* (1842; repr., New York: Wiley and Putnam, 1846), 78.
3. See www.sistersofcharityolm.org.
4. St. Vincent's Academy, Savannah, Expenditures, 1845–1858, 943.002 #2, Mercy Heritage Center, Sisters of Mercy of the Americas, Belmont, North Carolina.
5. *The Metropolitan Catholic Almanac and Laity's Directory for the Year of Our Lord 1853* (Baltimore: Fielding Lucas Jr., 1853), 152–53.

Ellen LEONARD

On the Love of Retirement

Oh peace my repose long long have I wandered
And sought for that rest which may quiet my heart
But whilst I pursued life's checquered paths covered
The phantom of bliss but excited the smart
The soft dreams of pleasure the prospect may brighten
The cup they will gild but the poisen infuse
Alas the false sleep ere long shall awaken
When stripped of its magic twill cease to amuse
Thy waves may roll on tempestuous and stormy
Secure in the haven their rage I defy
No thougt save of pity shall ever come from me
Compassion alone shall e'er steal a sigh
What thanks then to GOD to be snatched from the billows
With which passion and pleasure deluge the soul
To discover a haven of bliss 'mid the shallows"
Each want to relieve each grief to console
Adieu then O world farewell to thy pleasures
No never again shall I mix in thy rounds
Too long had thy follies held me in fetters
Reflection surprises remembrance confounds.

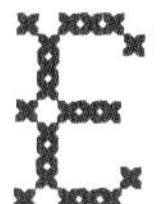
llen Leonard was among St. Vincent Academy's earliest students. The Savannah house of the Sisters of Mercy began accepting student tuitions for the academy in late June of 1845; Ellen completed her

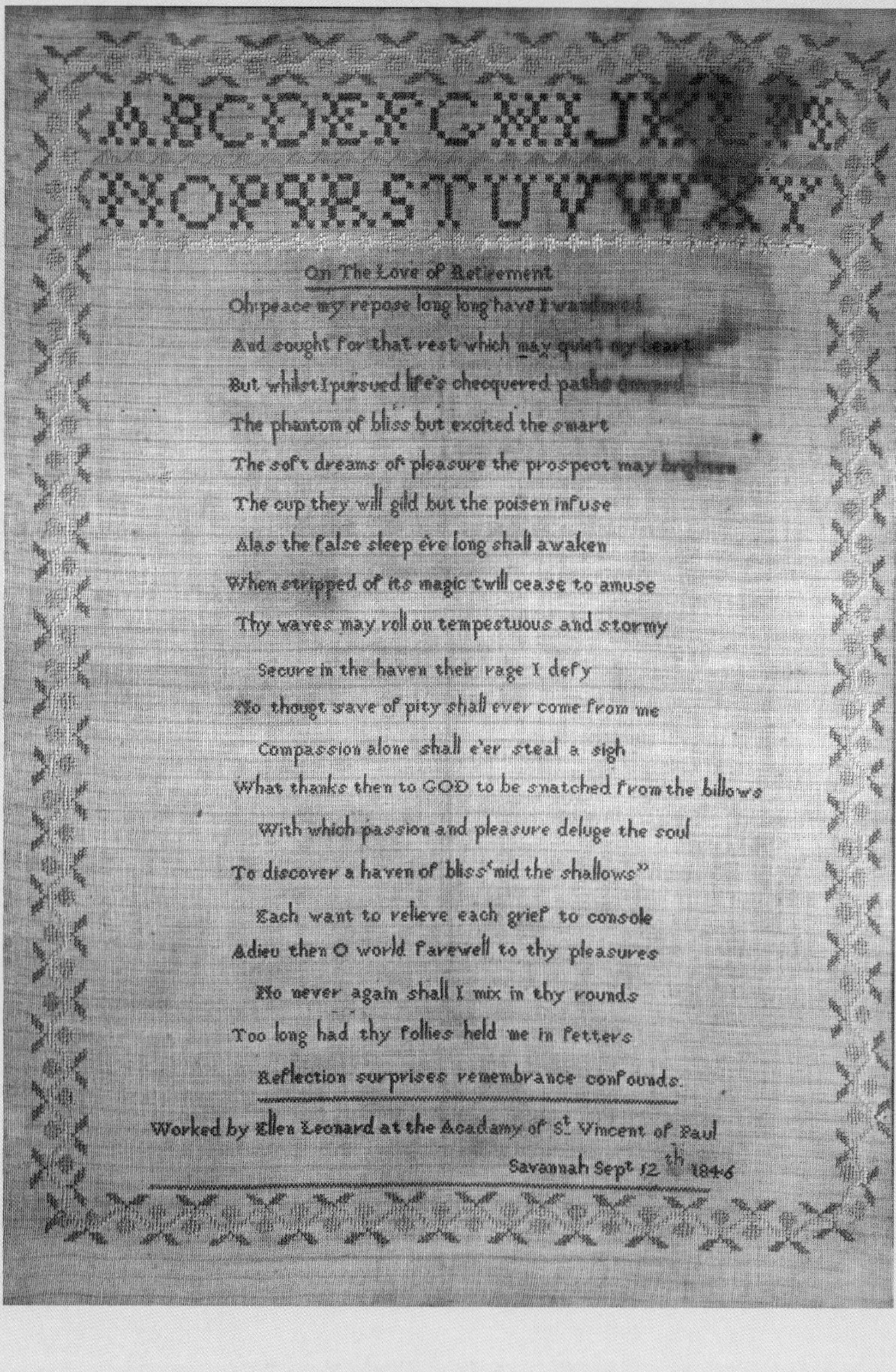

ABCDEFGHIJKLM

NOPQRSTUVWXY

On The Love of Retirement

Oh peace my repose long long have I wandered
And sought for that rest which may quiet my heart
But whilst I pursued life's chequered paths onward
The phantom of bliss but excited the smart
The soft dreams of pleasure the prospect may brighten
The cup they will gild but the poisen infuse
Alas the false sleep ere long shall awaken
When stripped of its magic twill cease to amuse
Thy waves may roll on tempestuous and stormy
Secure in the haven their rage I defy
No thougt save of pity shall ever come from me
Compassion alone shall e'er steal a sigh
What thanks then to GOD to be snatched from the billows
With which passion and pleasure deluge the soul
To discover a haven of bliss 'mid the shallows
Each want to relieve each grief to console
Adieu then O world farewell to thy pleasures
No never again shall I mix in thy rounds
Too long had thy follies held me in fetters
Reflection surprises remembrance confounds.

Worked by Ellen Leonard at the Acadamy of St. Vincent of Paul

Savannah Sept 12th 1846

sampler a year later. For the pre-Civil War period 1845–1860, tuition ranged from three to ten dollars per three-month session, the monetary differences likely reflecting the number and/or kinds of subjects each girl studied.[1] The sisters made local purchases of needlework supplies, including silk floss, ribbon and tape, wool yarn, canvas, papers of pins, and needles.[2]

Ellen's name is not among those whose parents or guardians paid for tuition, nor does the surname Leonard appear in the academy's receipt book. The latter book is peppered, however, with entries for donations to "the orphan fund," "from the church's orphan fund," and "for the Orphans." It is probable that Ellen Leonard was either parentless or the daughter of a single parent who could not provide for her. She was fortunate, however, to receive care as well as an education from the Sisters of Mercy.

Ellen's name is not among those whose parents or guardians paid for tuition, nor does the surname Leonard appear in the academy's receipt book.

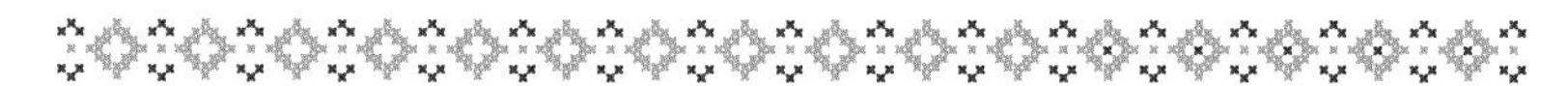

"On the Love of Retirement," a poem peppered with both obscure references and well-worn phrases, does not appear to have a published source. Ellen is unlikely to have penned the verses, but perhaps the composition originated with one of her teachers. She may also have been asked, as an exercise in English composition, to take a passage of published prose and convert it to rhyme.

Ellen's sampler was given to St. Vincent's Academy; the circumstances of the gift are unrecorded.

Embroidered sampler by Ellen Leonard, dated September 12, 1846. Worked at the Academy of St. Vincent of Paul, Savannah, Chatham County. Two-ply twisted silk thread on balanced plain weave linen with colored thread woven every tenth thread in the weft. Stitches: counted cross over 1 x 1 and 2 x 2 threads; square eyelet over 4 x 4 threads. 25 x 18 1/2 inches (framed). Collection of St. Vincent's Academy, Savannah, Georgia

NOTES

1. St. Vincent's Academy, Savannah, Tuition Book, June 1845–April 1870, 946.005, Mercy Heritage Center, Sisters of Mercy of the Americas, Belmont, North Carolina (here after cited as Mercy Heritage Center).
2. For example, payment to Mary Dillon, October 31, 1845, St. Vincent's Academy, Savannah, Expenditures, 1845–1858, 943.002 #2, Mercy Heritage Center; and payment to Mrs. Doer, March 27, 1847, St. Vincent's Academy, Savannah, Expenditures, 1845–1858, 943.002 #2, Mercy Heritage Center.

No. 11

Mary Teresa KERLEY

Hymn
To the Blessed Virgin

As the dewy shades of even
Gather o'er the balmy air
Listen gentle Queen of Heaven
Listen to my vesper prayer

Holy Mother near me hover
Free my thoughts from aught defiled.
With thy wings of mercy cover
Keep from sin thy helpless child

Thine own sinless heart was broken
Sorrow's sword had pierced the core
Holy Mother by that token
Now thy pity I implore.

Queen of Heaven guard and guide me
Save my soul from dark despair
In thy tender bosom hide me
Take me mother to thy care.

Mary Kerley's father, Nicholas (ca. 1802–1854), came to the United States in about 1828 as one of the hundreds of Irish immigrants who poured into New York after the conclusion of the War of 1812. A son, Michael, was born there in 1831 (the mother's name

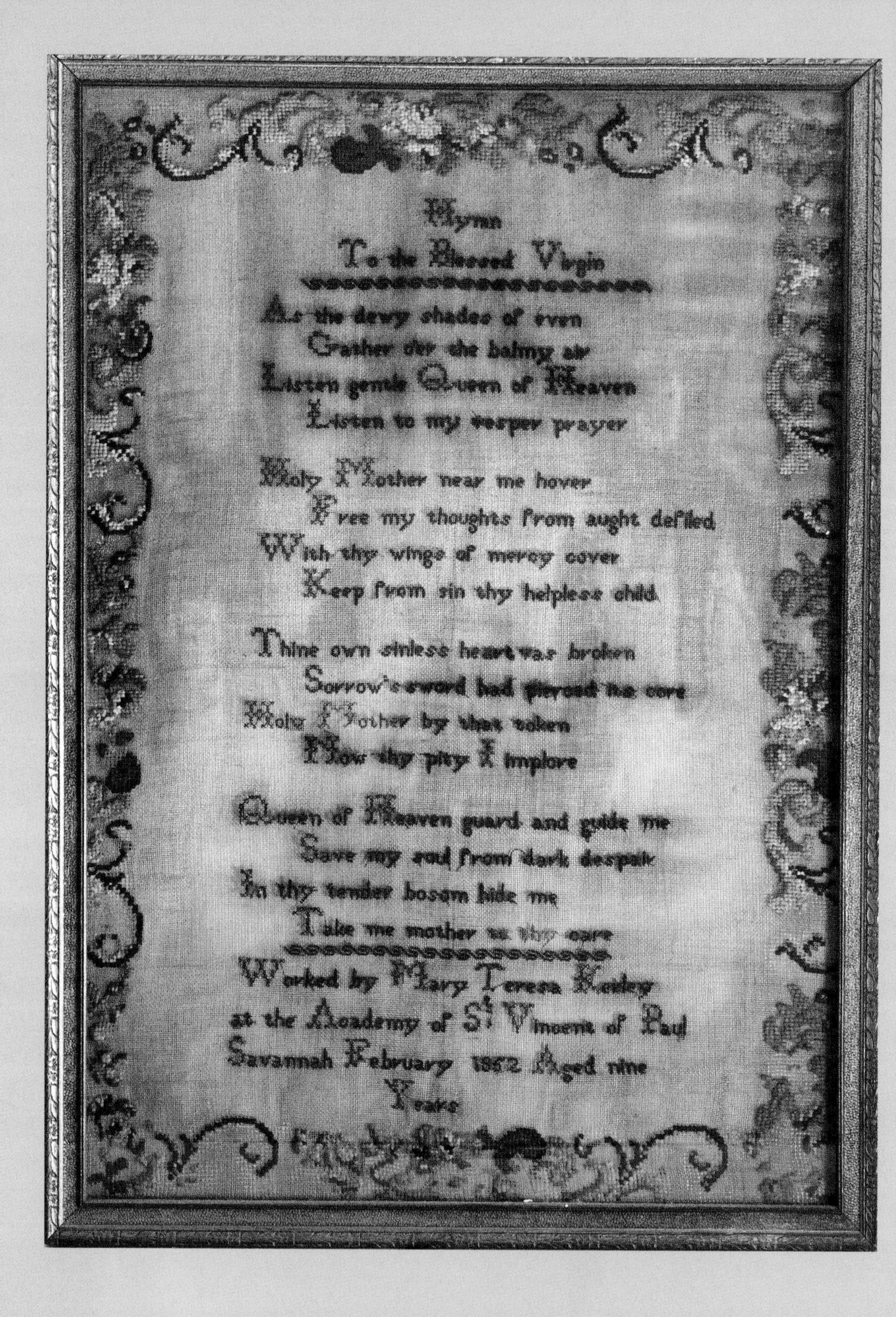
Hymn
To the Blessed Virgin
As the dewy shades of even
Gather o'er the balmy air
Listen gentle Queen of Heaven
Listen to my vesper prayer
Holy Mother near me hover
Free my thoughts from aught defiled
With thy wings of mercy cover
Keep from sin thy helpless child
Thine own sinless heart was broken
Sorrow's sword had pierced its core
Holy Mother by that token
Now thy pity I implore
Queen of Heaven guard and guide me
Save my soul from dark despair
In thy tender bosom hide me
Take me mother to thy care
Worked by Mary Teresa Keiley
at the Academy of St Vincent of Paul
Savannah February 1862 Aged nine
Years

is unknown), and Nicholas was naturalized as a US citizen in 1833, at the Marine Court in New York City. He gave his occupation as house carpenter.[1]

Greater economic opportunities must have lured Nicholas south; in about 1840, he left one urban area for another, resettling, with Michael, in Savannah.[2] Unlike Georgia's Scots-Irish, who came from an Ulster Presbyterian background and had established themselves before the 1820s as property owners, the Irish Catholics who arrived in the antebellum era were attracted by construction projects, including canals and railways. Many of them joined the menial labor force in Savannah, making do in the neighborhoods of cramped quarters that skirted the city.

Nicholas met and married Bridget Dunn (ca. 1815–1861) in Savannah in 1841. The two may have lived in the same neighborhood or they might have encountered each other at the Church of St. John the Baptist, Savannah's only Catholic church. Their daughter, Mary Teresa, was born about 1843. Lawsuits in which Nicholas was the plaintiff for the collection of money suggest that he was actively practicing a trade in the 1840s. One of his clients was St. Vincent's Academy, and he was intermittently in its employ as a carpenter from 1845 through 1852.[3]

Tax records suggest that the Kerley family lived in rented quarters until about 1850, when the family's finances improved. In that year, the family was living in Currytown, the southwesternmost section of Savannah, in an "improvement"—likely a small dwelling that Nicholas might have constructed himself—valued at five hundred dollars, on land owned by a G. W. Dillon.[4] The family's neighbors, living in the surrounding wooden tenements and boarding houses, were free and enslaved workers as well as foreigners and citizens.

Embroidered sampler by Mary Teresa Kerley (born ca. 1843), dated February 1852. Worked at the Academy of St. Vincent of Paul, Savannah, Chatham County. Two-ply silk thread and merino wool on balanced plain weave linen. Stitches: counted cross over 1 x 1 and 2 x 2 threads. 21 x 15 inches (framed). Collection of St. Vincent's Academy, Savannah, Georgia

In October 1849, Mary Teresa Kerley was enrolled as a day student at St. Vincent's Academy, and her father paid five dollars for three months' tuition.[5] Mary's commute, undoubtedly on foot, was several miles each way. Her education must have been a financial priority; her parents made regular tuition payments from January 1850 through the end of December 1852.

She surrounded the hymn's four verses and a personal inscription—her name, age, school, and date of completion—with colorful flowers and spider-leg scrolls, which she likely copied or adapted from a printed source.

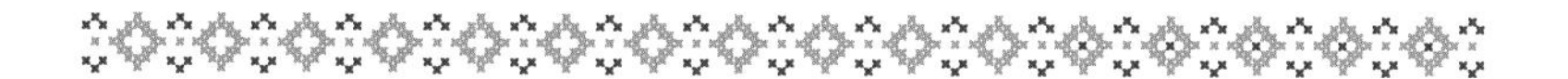

In February of 1852, at the age of nine, Mary completed a sampler, the subject of which was a "Hymn To the Blessed Virgin." This devotional had been published in the *United States Catholic Magazine and Monthly Review* in 1847.[6] She surrounded the hymn's four verses and a personal inscription—her name, age, school, and date of completion—with colorful flowers and spider-leg scrolls, which she likely copied or adapted from a printed source.

Although Mary continued to attend St. Vincent's Academy, her enrollment during the following three years was erratic: one or two terms in 1853, three terms in 1854, and one term in 1855. In 1854, Bridget Kerley paid five dollars for her daughter to take one quarter's worth of lessons with the academy's music teacher, Miss McNulty.[7] The beginning of this change coincides with Nicholas's absence in the academy's expenditure ledger, all hinting at a reversal in the family's financial stability.

In the summer and fall of 1854, Savannah experienced the second of three major yellow fever epidemics that broke out in the city during the nineteenth century.[8] A hemorrhagic virus carried by the female of a mosquito species native to Africa, yellow fever thrived in the climate of southern states, and those who worked outside were especially at risk during epidemics. In Savannah, poor sanitation and crowded conditions impeded recovery among the working poor. Nicholas Kerley was one of the 1,040 inhabitants who succumbed to the disease at the end of September; he was buried in Savannah's Catholic Cemetery.

Bridget was named executrix of her husband's estate. Nicholas's outstanding debts, amounting to hundreds of dollars, required multiple appearances in court and must have exhausted her remaining resources. For example, in 1855, she was ordered to pay, either from the estate or from her own property, $105 plus interest and court charges to plaintiff Peter L. Constantine; the recording clerk noted, "the said defendant in Mercy [i.e., threw herself upon the mercy of the court]."[9] She managed to hold onto the dwelling in Currytown, which in 1856 was worth six hundred dollars.[10] In August 1861, Bridget died of "jaundice" (liver disease) and was also buried in Savannah's Catholic Cemetery.

Mary's fate is currently unknown. She disappeared from St. Vincent's Academy records after 1855, and her name does not appear in federal census records after 1850. Her sampler was given to St. Vincent's Academy, but details surrounding the gift were not recorded.

NOTES

1. Nicholas Kerley, United States Naturalization Record Indexes, 1791–1992, Ancestry.com.
2. According to the 1850 United States Federal Census, nineteen-year-old Michael worked as a mason. For a broader look at Irish settlement in the American South, see David T. Gleeson, *The Irish in the South, 1815–1877* (Chapel Hill: University of North Carolina Press, 2001).
3. St. Vincent's Academy, Savannah, Expenditures, 1845–1858, 943.002 #2, Mercy Heritage Center, Sisters of Mercy of the Americas, Belmont, North Carolina (hereafter cited as Mercy Heritage Cen-

ter). Besides unspecified carpentry work, Nicholas was paid for constructing five benches, boxes, and a desk in May 1851.

4. Nicholas Kerly, Savannah, Georgia, tax digest, 1850, Ancestry.com. The reason for the different spelling of his surname on this record is unknown.
5. St. Vincent's Academy, Savannah; Tuition Book, June 1845–April 1870, 946.005, Mercy Heritage Center, and Receipts of Tuition, Board, Donations, etc. 1845–July 1858, 943.001, Mercy Heritage Center.
6. "Hymn to the Blessed Virgin," vol. 6 of *United States Catholic Magazine and Monthly Review* (Baltimore: John Murphy, 1847), 567–68, http://hdl.handle.net/2027/njp.32101067868834. The verses were set to music by a Professor Dielman.
7. St. Vincent's Academy, Savannah, Tuition Book, June 1845–April 1870, 946.005, Mercy Heritage Center, and Receipts of Tuition, Board, Donations, etc., 1845–July 1858, 943.001, Mercy Heritage Center.
8. The first swept the city in 1820, resulting in the deaths of 666 inhabitants; the third developed in 1876 and killed more than one thousand residents.
9. Peter L. Constantine vs. Bridget Kerley, executrix, Nicholas Kerley, 12 May 1855, City of Savannah Court Record Books, 1855, Ancestry.com.
10. Mrs. Bridget Kerley, Chatham County, Georgia, tax digest, 1856, Ancestry.com.

Catherine WALLACE

Hymn To the Blessed Virgin

Hail Mary Queen and Virgin pure
With every grace replete
Hail kind protectress of the poor
Pity our needy state

O thou who fillest the highest place
Near heavens imperial throne
Obtain for us each saving grace
And make our wants thy own

How oft when trouble fill'd my breast
Or sin my conscience pain'd
Through thee I sought for peace and rest
Through thee I peace obtain'd

According to the school's carefully kept tuition ledger, Catherine Wallace attended St. Vincent's Academy as a boarding student for the whole of 1852, for one three-month session as a day scholar between 1853 and the first half of 1854, and as a boarder again between July 1854 and July 1855.[1] The first year's quarterly charges, totaling $120, were paid promptly. The expenses for 1853–55, totaling $75, were not fully discharged until 1862. The irregularities of both Catherine's attendance and her tuition and boarding payments for these three years hint strongly at devastating change in the Wallace household—perhaps the loss of a parent or

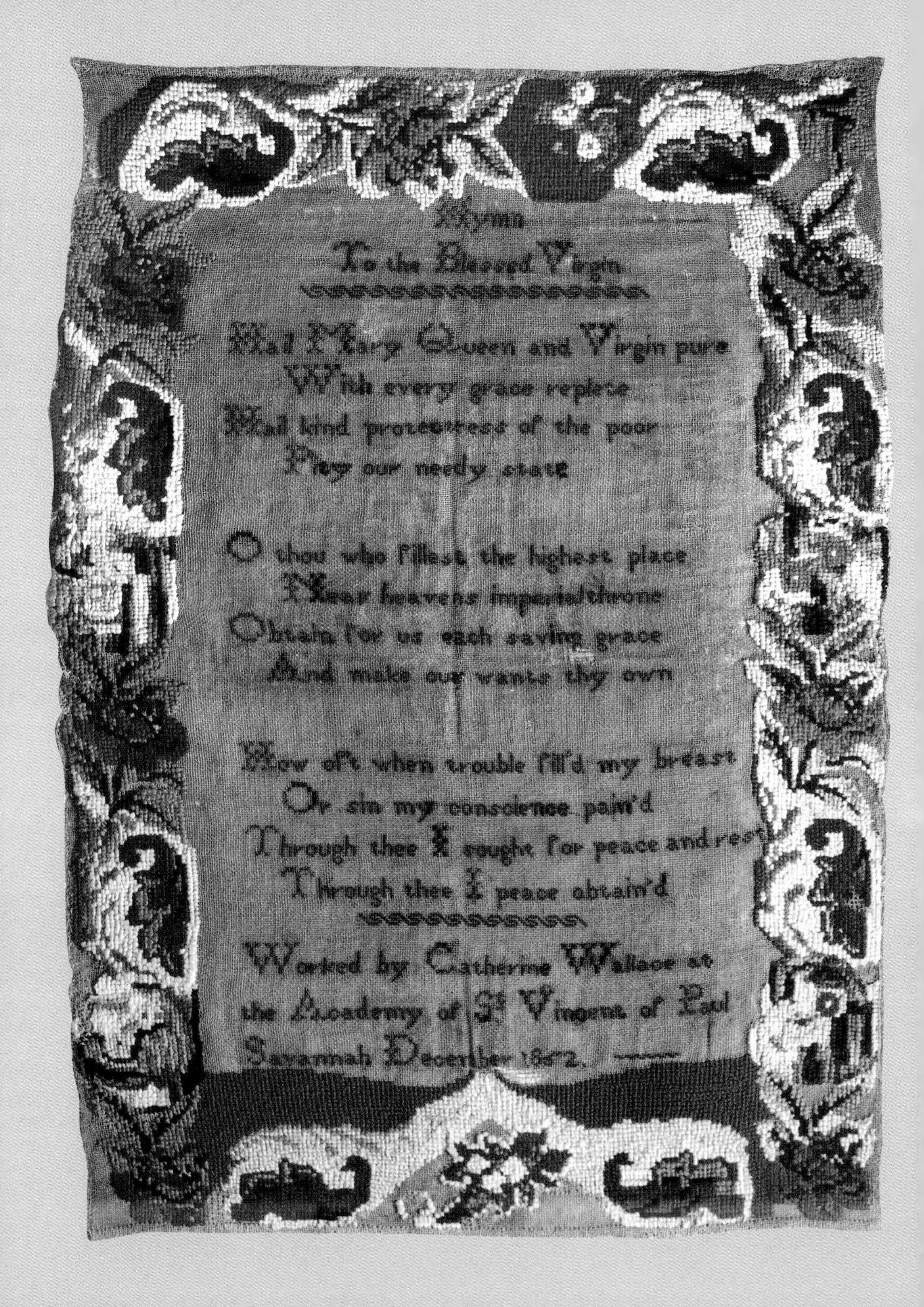
Hymn
To the Blessed Virgin
Hail Mary Queen and Virgin pure
With every grace replete
Hail kind protectress of the poor
Pity our needy state
O thou who fillest the highest place
Near heavens imperial throne
Obtain for us each saving grace
And make our wants thy own
How oft when trouble fill'd my breast
Or sin my conscience pain'd
Through thee I sought for peace and rest
Through thee I peace obtain'd
Worked by Catherine Wallace at
the Academy of St Vincent of Paul
Savannah December 1862.

her father's livelihood. Census and court records have yet to reveal information on the Wallace family.

Catherine might have fashioned the colorful woolwork floral border on her sampler following a charted design. The lack of subtle coloring in the flowers and leaves suggests that the pattern was drawn as a detailed outline onto the fabric; she would have been responsible for color placement and shading.

The lack of subtle coloring in the flowers and leaves suggests that the pattern was drawn as a detailed outline onto the fabric . . .

St. Vincent's Academy procured embroidery designs and needlework supplies from several sources. For example, in March of 1850, a Mrs. Prendergast received forty dollars from the academy for "silver lace, ornaments, worsted, patterns &c. purchased by her in N. York." In June of 1851, the sisters paid an unknown local supplier for "worsted & patterns" and, in May of 1852, for "floss silk & patterns."[2] These entries in the academy's expenditure ledger constitute the first evidence of embroidery patterns acquired by the sisters. It is tempting to conclude that these patterns were charted designs suitable for sampler motifs and borders, but the sisters also constructed ecclesiastical garments, and the patterns may have been outline drawings for silkwork or whitework techniques.

Catherine's sampler was given to St. Vincent's Academy; the circumstances of the gift are unknown.

Embroidered sampler by Catherine Wallace, dated December 1852. Worked at the Academy of St. Vincent of Paul, Savannah, Chatham County. Two-ply twisted silk thread and wool yarn on balanced plain weave linen. Stitches: counted cross over 1 x 1 and 2 x 2 threads. 21 1/2 x 16 1/2 inches (framed). Collection of St. Vincent's Academy, Savannah, Georgia

NOTES

1. St. Vincent's Academy, Savannah, Tuition Book, June 1845–April 1870, 946.005, Mercy Heritage Center, Sisters of Mercy of the Americas, Belmont, North Carolina (hereafter cited as Mercy Heritage Center).
2. St. Vincent's Academy, Savannah, Expenditures, 1845–1858, 943.002 #2, Mercy Heritage Center.

Caroline Broughton FABIAN

The death of George Washington, on December 14, 1799, produced an extraordinary outpouring of public emotion in the United States.[1] Washington had been a popular figure during the last two decades of his life; his likeness was portrayed repeatedly in woodcut prints and on utilitarian articles—textiles, metalwork, ceramics, and glass—manufactured primarily in England after the end of the Revolutionary War. His death sparked an increase in this specialized trade. Foreign as well as domestic manufacturers tailored commemorative goods for an expanding American middle class: American and English printers published engravings, many of which were based on paintings; images were sent to China to copy as hand-painted portraits on porcelain; English ceramics manufacturers made creamware with transfer prints; and England's textile manufacturers continued production of the copperplate-printed furnishing fabrics (toiles) featuring Washington's image created during his lifetime.

Newspapers and broadsides featured elegies in prose and verse. A visiting Russian diplomat, Pavel Svinin, observed as late as 1811, "every American considers it his sacred duty to have a likeness of Washington in his home just as we have images of God's saints. . . . Washington's portrait is the finest and sometime the sole decoration of American homes."[2] These memorial depictions and descriptions of Washington were of two forms: Washington mourned as the war hero and the country's first leader, "a great and good man"; and the immortal Washington, ascending to heaven.[3]

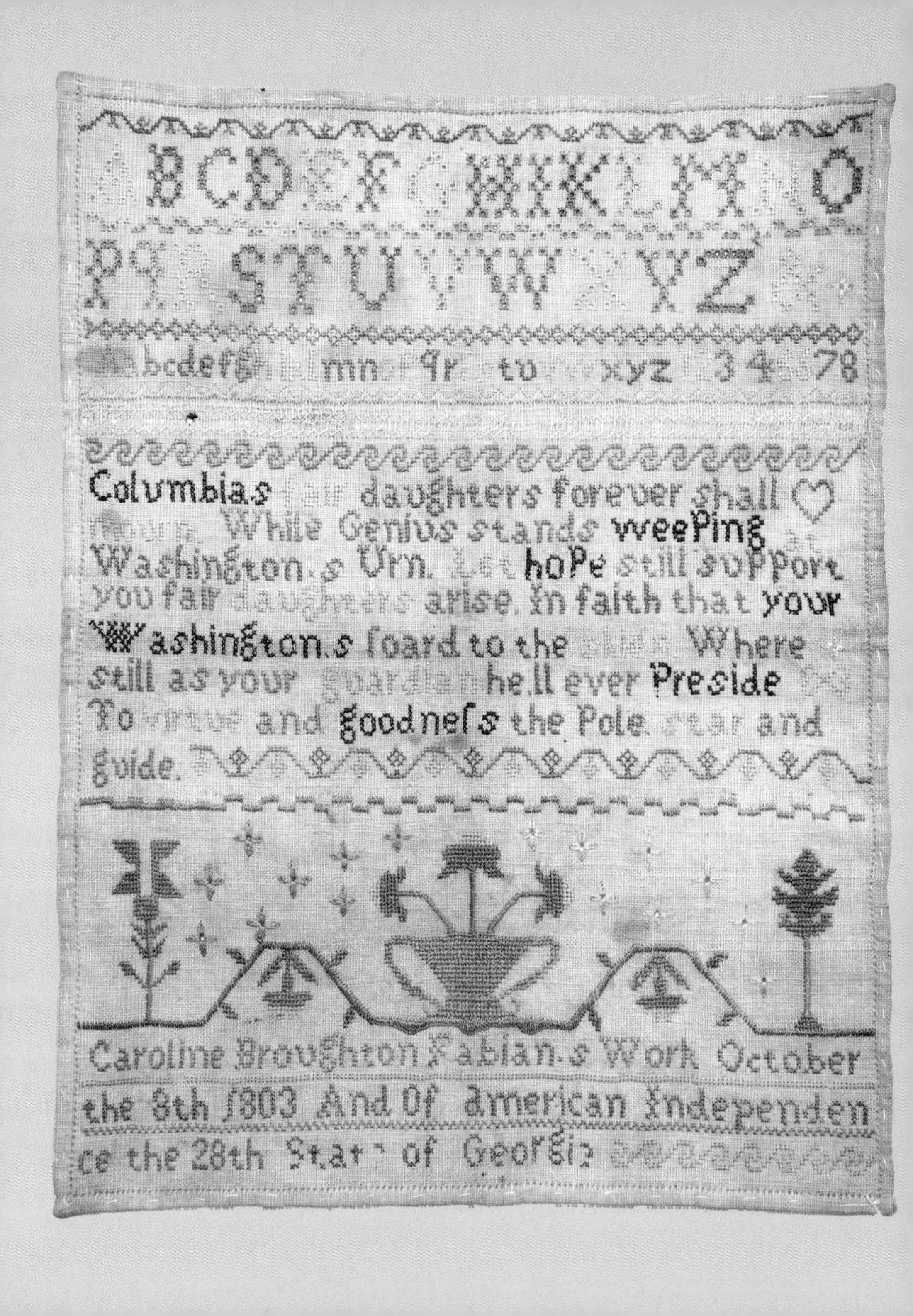
Columbias fair daughters forever shall mourn While Genius stands weeping at
Washington.s Urn. Let hope still support
you fair daughters arise. In faith that your
Washington.s soard to the skies Where
still as your guardian he.ll ever Preside
To virtue and goodness the Pole star and
guide.
Caroline Broughton Fabian.s Work October
the 8th 1803 And Of American Independen
ce the 28th State of Georgia

Among the earliest and most decorative of these material expressions of grief were mourning pictures worked by young girls. The majority of these are elaborate scenes, most of them memorials to the secular leader, embroidered in silk threads and/or painted in watercolors on a satin-woven silk ground. In contrast to these elegant funerary compositions, Caroline Broughton Fabian's memorial to Washington is a sampler. The embroidery features two alphabets, numbers, horizontal bands of patterns, and two inscriptions.

The first inscription is the apotheosis of mourning for Washington in verse, copied from an anonymous author. It originally appeared, with a prescriptive heading, in the July 15, 1800, issue of the *New Hampshire Gazette* (Portsmouth):

> *LINES For a Miss, to work under an* URN of WASHINGTON
> COLUMBIA'S fair daughters forever shall mourn
> While Genius stands weeping at WASHINGTON'S Urn.
> Let hope still support you, fair daughters arise
> In faith that your WASHINGTON'S soar'd to the skies,
> Where still as your guardian he'll ever preside
> To virtue and goodness the pole star and guide.[4]

This verse was not published in any of Savannah's newspapers, but it may have been sent south as a clipping from northern friends or relations or circulated locally as a broadside. Caroline's prose inscription is equally patriotic; in addition to her name and date of completion—October 8, 1803—she reminded her viewers that 1803 was "the 28th" year "of American Independence." She ended with a declaration of her residence: "State of Georgia."

John C. Fabian (ca. 1730–after 1801), Caroline's father, established himself as a planter on St. Simons Island sometime before the Revolutionary War;

Embroidered sampler-style memorial to George Washington by Caroline Broughton Fabian (1792–1854), dated October 8, 1803. Worker's residence: St. Simons Island, Glynn County. Two-ply twisted silk thread on balanced plain weave linen; edges turned under twice and hemstitched. Stitches: counted cross over 2 x 2 threads; square eyelet over 4 x 4 threads; counted satin. 12 5/8 x 9 3/4 inches. Collection of the Charleston Museum; Gift of Mrs. Lorene Davis Argoe, 1957. Acc. no. HT 517

in about 1775 he married Mary Ann Broughton (ca. 1757–1830). Nothing is known about Fabian's activities during the war, but most of the island's landowners were Whig sympathizers.[5] In the 1790s, Fabian likely switched to growing long-staple cotton (known today as sea island cotton). Records indicate that in 1792 he borrowed slaves from William McIntosh for planting in exchange for a portion of the crop.[6] Caroline was born November 12 of that year.

Among the earliest and most decorative of these material expressions of grief were mourning pictures worked by young girls.

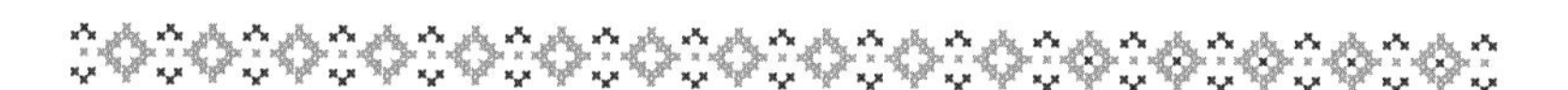

Caroline was in South Carolina by 1827, when she married William Cardinal Davis (1804–after 1860), a planter with small holdings and, in 1840, three enslaved field hands.[7] The couple had two daughters and a son. The sampler descended from Caroline to her daughter-in-law, Susan Caroline Phillips Davis, to Susan's daughter, Emma L. Davis Argoe. Emma presented the sampler to the Charleston Museum in 1957.

NOTES

1. Many of Georgia's citizens publicly grieved the death of Washington. On January 7, 1800, Savannah's newspaper, the *Columbian Museum*, reported that the mayor and aldermen of the city would wear "deep mourning for one month," and the city council recommended "that the merchants, shop-keepers, and tradesmen in this city, do shut up their stores and shops for three days [January 6–8] . . . as mark of respect to the memory that illustrious character."
2. Pavel Petrovich Svinin, *Picturesque United States of America: 1811, 1812, 1813* (New York: William Edwin Rudge, 1930), 34, quoted in Barbara J. Mitnick, "Parallel Visions: The Literary and Visual Image of George Washington," in Barbara J. Mitnick, ed., *George Washington: American Symbol* (New York: Hudson Hills Press, 1999), 59.
3. For a full discussion of the commercialization of Washington's image, see Mitnick.

4. Quoted in Davida Tenenbaum Deutsch, "Washington Memorial Prints," *The Magazine Antiques* 111, no. 2 (February 1977): 325, figure 2. The Rhode Island Historical Society owns another sampler with this verse, also dated 1800, worked by Lucy Child. It includes a tree overhanging a tomb marked "G. W." and surmounted by an urn bearing a Masonic emblem.
5. Memorial of John Fabian, 1783, John Fabian Papers, file 244, #44, Georgia Historical Society, Savannah, Georgia.
6. William Mackintosh to his father Lachlan McIntosh, St. Simons, Georgia, 1792 November 8, folder 5, Correspondence and Other Papers, 1785–1799, Lachlan McIntosh Papers, MS 0526, Georgia Historical Society, Savannah, Georgia; and Agreement between John Fabian and William McIntosh Jr., 1792 December 20, folder 5, Correspondence and Other Papers, 1785–1799, Lachlan McIntosh Papers.
7. William C. Davis, 1840 Federal Census, St. Johns Parish, Colleton, South Carolina, Ancestry.com.

Olivia Winifred JORDAN

Olivia Jordan was born into the third generation of a large extended family whose strong ties of kinship "both as friend and relative" informed decisions on migration and resettlement.[1] Even her name reflects this legacy: Olivia for the worker's maternal grandmother, Olivia Ball, and Winifred for her paternal grandmother, Winifred Jordan.

John Jordan (1758–1828), the family's patriarch and Olivia's grandfather, was born in a part of Brunswick County, Virginia, that in 1781 was established as Greensville County. Aunts, uncles, cousins, and cousins many times removed were scattered throughout Greensville as well as Northampton County, North Carolina, which shares much of its northern border with Greensville. From about the mid-1770s until after 1800, John worked as an overseer on a number of plantations, most of which were owned by his relations.[2] In 1786, he married his second cousin, Winifred Jordan (1763–1847), who was living in Northampton.

John was close to another cousin, Jesse Jordan. In 1791, Jesse married Janet Hayley, the daughter of Henry Hayley, one of John's employers. Janet recollected decades later that, when she and Jesse moved to another part of Greensville, John "purchased a place within two miles" of the couple; and when "Jesse Jordan moved to Georgia and settled in Washington County [about 1798], . . . that a few years afterwards [about 1804] the said John and wife [Winifred] moved to the same State and County and the

---

Embroidered sampler by Olivia Winifred Jordan (1818–1866), ca. 1828. Worker's residence: Washington County. Two-ply twisted silk thread on balanced plain weave linen; selvages at right and left; top and bottom edges turned under twice and hemmed. Stitches: counted cross over 1 x 1 and 2 x 2 threads; square eyelet over 4 x 4 threads; four-sided stitch over 2 x 2 threads. 15 7/8 x 17 1/8 inches. Georgia Museum of Art, University of Georgia; Museum purchase with funds provided by the Board of Advisors in memory of Shara Overstreet. GMOA 2010.80

abcdefghijklmnopqrstuvwxyz
Olivia Winefred Jordans work.

two families have resided within from two to four miles of each other." Janet characterized this relationship as living "in intimacy," explaining that Henry Hayley and John Jordan were cousins and Jesse Jordan and Winifred Jordan were cousins.[3]

. . . Olivia must have felt a longing for close female companionship: the girls' mother had died in 1840, the eldest daughter, Ann, had married in 1836, and now Mary Ann had left home.

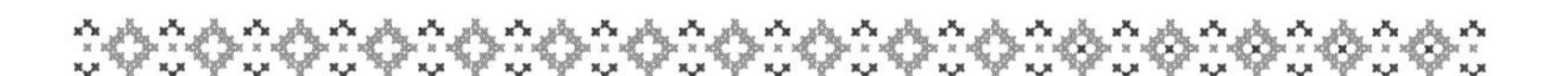

Britton Jordan (1787–1826), Olivia's father, was the eldest of the seven children John and Winifred brought to Washington County. The house, thought to have been built as a temporary residence for the family, still stands: a dogtrot cabin constructed with squared, notched logs, with a steep roof and chimneys on the gabled ends.[4] Father and son became successful slave-owning planters and likely raised cotton and/or engaged in wool production.

In 1813, Britton married Margaret Josey Bell (1790–1860). Olivia was the third of seven children born to the couple. She was only eight years old when her father died, and she likely had not yet begun work on her sampler. According to his will, Britton left his family well provided for, and all of his children inherited additional money and property upon the death of their grandfather two years later.[5]

In 1843, Olivia's younger sister, Mary Ann (1821–1859), married Jesse Batts (b. 1818), and the couple moved to Barbour County, Alabama. Batts became a wealthy corn and rice planter; in 1850, his plantation was worth $11,000 and he owned seventy-two slaves.[6] Mary Ann's inheritance likely contributed to this success. At the time of her sister's marriage, Olivia must have felt a longing for close female companionship: the girls' mother had died in 1840, the eldest daughter, Ann, had married in 1836, and now Mary Ann had left home. By 1850, Olivia was living with Jesse, Mary Ann, and the couple's two young children.

In the 1850s, the family and Olivia headed west again, this time to Brazos County, Texas.[7] Located in the southern portion of central Texas, the area had a mixed economy of small farms in cotton and corn production and a railroad line to Houston. Jesse farmed with the aid of forty-seven bondspeople and operated a ferry across the Brazos River in the southern part of the county.[8] Mary Ann died in 1859; on March 29, 1860, Jesse and Olivia married. Olivia's inheritance would have passed legally to Jesse with this marriage, but she may have combined her resources with her sister's in the 1840s. Olivia died childless six years later.

NOTES

1. Sworn statement of Jincey (Janet) Hayley Jordan Riddle, Pension W29726, Revolutionary War Pension and Bounty-Land Warrant Application Files, National Archives and Records Administration (NARA), Fold3.com (hereafter cited as Pension W29276).
2. Although John Jordan never applied for a Revolutionary War pension, he told family and friends that between 1779 and 1781 he had fought under General Samuel Elbert at the siege of Savannah, was taken prisoner and lived aboard a British prison ship for over three months, returned home to recover from the experience, and then rejoined his militia for the surrender of Cornwallis at Yorktown. No military records have survived to support this claim. In 1846, his widow, Winifred, applied for a widow's pension. Her claim of his service was supported by several sworn witnesses, all members of the couple's extended family. A John Jordan was found to have served under a Captain Pendleton of Harrison's Artillery, and another John Jordan received a warrant for one hundred acres of land in Virginia for his service. The family was unable to prove that Winifred's husband was either one of these servicemen, and her application was denied. In 1889, John and Winifred's only surviving child, Mary Jordan Newton, of Athens, Georgia, applied for and received, under a special act of Congress, a small pension, which she collected until her death, in 1893. In this case, no new proof of service was provided, and John was listed on the paperwork as a member of the Continental Line in the Revolution but with no details of that service. It is interesting to note that, in this case, Mary's supporter was her son-in-law, US Congressman from Athens Henry Hull Carlton. See Pension W29726.

3. Pension W29726. Sworn statement of Jincey (Janet) Hayley Jordan Riddle.
4. John Linley, *Architecture of Middle Georgia; The Oconee Area* (Athens: University of Georgia Press, 2014), 24.
5. Research notes, registration file for Olivia Jordan's sampler, Georgia Museum of Art, Athens, Georgia.
6. 1850 Federal Non-Population Schedules and Slave Schedules, Division 23, Barbour, Alabama, Ancestry.com.
7. Jesse Batts was on the Brazos County tax rolls in 1859 and 1860.
8. Jesse Batts, 1860 Federal Census Slave Schedules, Precinct 1, Brazos, Texas, Brazos County Commissioners Minutes, Book B, 209, Ancestry.com.

Martha STRONG

Located in northeast Georgia and named for the colony's founder, James Edward Oglethorpe, Oglethorpe County was established in 1793. The area was created out of Wilkes County, and the tracts lay in the large region of land ceded to Georgia by the Creek and Cherokee nations in 1773. The first wave of post–Revolutionary War migration to the area brought families from older tobacco-producing sections of Virginia, lured by the prospect of fresh acreage for cultivation and Georgia's liberal land policy. Most of the men were small planters, and many were war veterans. In 1785, anticipating the growth of the tobacco trade, the Georgia legislature established a comprehensive tobacco inspection system that included an inspection warehouse at the town of Petersburg, situated on the Broad River in Wilkes County. By the turn of the century, Oglethorpe County had at least one inspection center of its own.[1]

Among the settlers in Oglethorpe County were Charles (1763–1848) and Sarah Thompson (1764–1849) Strong. Born in Hanover County, in the piedmont of Virginia, Charles was living in Goochland County in 1781 when he was called into the Virginia militia to serve the first of three tours of duty, the last of which was to guard the military stores during the siege at Yorktown.[2] After the war, Charles returned to Goochland County and, on November 25, 1785, married Sarah Thompson.[3] Almost immediately the couple moved southwest to Cumberland County, Virginia, where six of their children were born.

ABCDEFGHIJKLMNOP
Martha Strong.s sampler April 23.1818 Georgia.

According to Charles's sworn testimony for his Revolutionary War pension, he resettled the family in Georgia in 1800, near Cherokee Corner, an area on the central western edge of Oglethorpe.[4] He built his house atop a hill at what is now Arnoldsville.[5] Charles may have established himself as a tobacco planter but, like many of his neighbors, likely switched to cotton in the late 1810s because tobacco production had exhausted the soil.[6]

Born November 7, 1805, Martha Strong was the second of three children Charles and Sarah had in Oglethorpe County.

Born November 7, 1805, Martha Strong was the second of three children Charles and Sarah had in Oglethorpe County. She was twelve and a half years old when she completed her marking sampler, which is characterized by rows of alphabets and distinguished by a panel of animals and spiky trees. She added a completion date, April 23, 1818, and named Georgia as her state of residence. Martha almost certainly attended Esther Finley's House for the Board and Education of Young Ladies in Bethlehem, a small, unincorporated area of Cherokee Corner with a post office of the same name.[7] As the Strong home was less than a mile away, Martha was likely a day student.

Esther Flynt Caldwell Finley (1763–1844) advertised her Bethlehem school the same year Martha completed her embroidery, noting that she employed experienced teachers and offered two tiers of subjects.[8] Needlework was included in the basic English tuition, along with writing, arithmetic, and the use of the globes, for fifteen dollars per session. Each session lasted twenty-three weeks. More expensive was "Natural and Moral Philosophy, Political Economy, Chemistry, with the principles of the Fine Arts," at twenty dollars

Embroidered sampler by Martha Strong (1805–1877), dated April 23, 1818. Worker's residence: Oglethorpe County; attributed to Mrs. Finley's School, Bethlehem, Oglethorpe County. Two-ply twisted silk threads on balanced plain weave linen; top and bottom edges turned under twice and hemmed; right and left sides hidden under frame lip. Stitches: counted cross over 2 x 2 threads; square eyelet over 4 x 4 threads. 13 5/8 x 14 5/8 inches (framed). Private collection

per session. Boarding, which included lodging, washing, fire, and candles, was an additional seventy-five dollars per session.[9]

In 1824, Martha married John Dortch Moss (1792–1864), a settler from Mecklenburg County, Virginia, who had served in the War of 1812.[10] At some point after the marriage, Moss purchased as a family residence the building that once housed Finley's school.[11] He became a wealthy Oglethorpe County planter with diversified agricultural production, and the couple had eight children. In 1860, his real estate was valued at over $11,000 and his personal estate at more than $37,000.[12]

Esther Flynt Caldwell Finley (1763–1844) advertised her Bethlehem school the same year that Martha completed her embroidery . . .

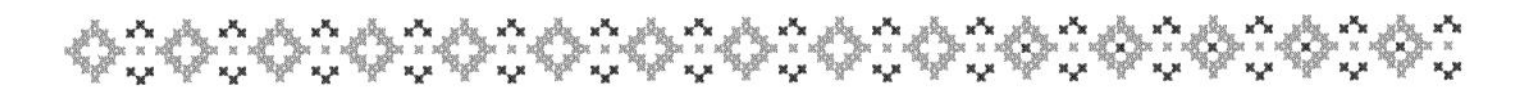

John and Martha lived in Athens, Georgia, in the 1860s. After John's death in 1864, Martha moved in with her eldest son, Rufus LaFayette Moss. A post–Civil War image of her survives (fig. 2). Martha died September 13, 1877; her sampler descended in the family to its present owner.

NOTES

1. G. Melvin Herndon, "Samuel Edward Butler of Virginia Goes to Georgia, 1784," *Georgia Historical Quarterly* 52, no. 2 (June 1968): 117–18.
2. Pension record of Charles Strong, Pension S.31994, Revolutionary War Pension and Bounty-Land Warrant Application Files, National Archives and Records Administration (NARA), Fold3.com.
3. About six months earlier, on March 21, Sarah Thompson's brother, John (1762–1810), married Charles's sister, Sarah (1767–after 1846). This couple immigrated to Georgia, settling in Clarke County; see Pension record of Sarah Thompson, R.10553, Revolutionary War Pension and Bounty-Land Warrant Application Files, NARA, Fold3.com.

Figure 2. Martha Strong Moss, carte de visite, unidentified photographer, ca. 1850–75. Private collection.

4. Pension record of Charles Strong. Cherokee Corner originally referred to an actual angle formed by two boundary lines—marked by a tree in 1775—of lands the Cherokee had ceded to Georgia; see *Historical Marker: Newsletter of Historic Oglethorpe County* 19, no. 2 (Fall 2009): 2.
5. Personal communication with Mary Bondurant Warren, June 11, 2015.
6. After the War of 1812, soil exhaustion led many planters either to search out more fertile lands westward or to shift to cotton production; see Herndon, 118.
7. Richard E. Small recorded a post office named Bethlehem, which was formerly called Cherokee Corner; see Richard E. Small, *The Post Offices of Georgia, 1764–1900* (n.p.: self-published, 1998), 2–5.
8. *Augusta (GA) Chronicle*, June 17, 1818.
9. The daughter of a Presbyterian minister, Esther was born in New Jersey and married Robert Finley (1772–1817) in Morristown. Robert graduated from Princeton in about 1787 and was licensed as a Presbyterian minister in 1794. The couple moved to Georgia in October of 1817 when Robert was hired as the University of Georgia's new president. He died three months after they arrived.
10. Index to Compiled Service Records of Volunteer Soldiers Who Served During the War of 1812, NARA, Fold3.com. John served as a sergeant in the 98th Regiment (Green's) of the Virginia Militia.
11. Personal communication with Mary Bondurant Warren, June 11, 2015. This property remained in the family until 1936.
12. John D. Moss, 1860 Federal Census, Athens, Clarke County, Georgia, Ancestry.com.

No. 16

Louisa ROGERS

Tis sweet on lofty Mountans brow
Where all is bright and all is fair
To hear the thunder peal below
And view the lighting flashing there.

O that to me the wings were given
That bear the Turtle to her nest.
Then would I cleave the vault of heav'n
And fly away and be at rest.

For roughly eight months in 1824, twenty-year-old Louisa Hanson Rogers resided in Asheville, North Carolina, with her maternal aunt and uncle, Caroline Lane (1761–1842) and George Charles Swain (1763–1829).[1] Her departure in March by carriage from her mother and younger siblings in Athens, Georgia, had been upsetting and hurried. Louisa's younger sister, Charlotte Paulette (b. 1807), was still beside herself in July, lamenting, "O my sister . . . there has not been a single night since I heard you were gone but what I have [cried]. . . . I go to the river [Oconee River] to your rock, repeat the name of my sister and I pray to the lord to protect you and return you to your home, why my sister O why did you go."[2]

On her part, Louisa was unsure about the future. On August 2, she penned "Reflections on Escaping the Mountains," in which she considered, "Five long months perhaps forever, / From the dearest friends to part."[3] Despite her uneasiness about home, she was enjoying herself in Asheville. She was loath

ABCDEFGHIJKLMNO
PQRSTUVWXYZ&12.
abcdefghijklmnopqrstuvwxyz 123456789
Tis sweet on lofty Mountans brow
Where all is bright and all is fair
To hear the thunder peal below
And view the lightning flashing there.
O that to me the wings were given
That bear the Turtle to her nest.
Then would I cleave the vault of heavn
And fly away and be at rest.
Wrought by
Louisa H. Rogers.
Asheville 1824.

to leave in October and composed a two-line verse to express her melancholy: "Farewell I come in bitterness of heart / To breathe that word of sadness and depart."[4] She scribbled lines to an unnamed cousin, describing her appreciation of the romantic beauty of the Asheville area—"lofty Mountains, flowry Meadows, chrytal stream[s], level farms, large fruit Orchards (on which the eye can rest with never ceasing delight)."[5]

Louisa likely crafted the first verse of the sampler's poetic inscription. She borrowed the second verse from the last four lines of Lord Byron's poem "I Would I Were a Careless Child," published in 1807.

Receiving and giving visits, answering correspondence, and traveling in the countryside likely occupied Louisa's days. Sometime during her stay—possibly with the guidance of an instructress—she stitched an elegant sampler featuring a two-story brick house with sash windows and two leafy shade trees. Louisa likely crafted the first verse of the sampler's poetic inscription. She borrowed the second verse from the last four lines of Lord Byron's poem "I Would I Were a Careless Child," published in 1807.

It is not possible to know what prompted Louisa to execute an embroidery form that most of her sex tackled as young girls. Her expressive verse and correspondence from this period testify to an academic education; however, she might not have been enrolled in "the ornamental branches" as a child. Perhaps her uncle now encouraged her. George Charles Swain was a trustee of Asheville's Female Academy, which had been established in 1810. It also is possible that whatever caused Louisa to leave her family was, upon

Embroidered sampler by Louisa Hanson Rogers (1804–1881), dated 1824. Worker's residence: Athens, Clarke County. Worked in: Asheville, Buncombe County, North Carolina. Two-ply twisted silk on balanced plain weave linen; edges turned under and hemmed; right edge is a selvage. Stitches: counted cross over 1 x 1 and 2 x 2 threads; queen over 4 x 4 threads; double running. 26 1/2 x 25 3/4 inches (framed). Collection of Carole Carpenter Wahler

reflection, an impetus for personal improvement and elevation of female accomplishments. The following year, in Athens, she engaged mapmaker Orange Green as a tutor to improve her penmanship.[6]

From about the age of thirteen, Louisa had enjoyed the attentions of local society; she saved five invitations she had received to parties and balls given in Athens, Lexington, and Watkinsville.[7] One can imagine that she also was attracting the attention of eligible young men. A comment from one of her male cousins intimates that, just prior to her Asheville visit, Louisa either snubbed or was rejected by an unnamed suitor. "Poor little fellow, tell her [Louisa] howdy and that she had been born to better stock."[8]

Louisa packed her sampler among her belongings as she prepared to return to Athens.[9] Once home, she settled into visits with family and friends and continued to write poetry. She still attracted attention. Between 1825 and her first marriage, in 1827, to James Cuthbert Steele, she had at least two serious admirers. One unknown gentleman (the signature was torn out from his letter) lived in McDonaugh, Henry County; the other was her penmanship teacher, Orange Green.[10]

An undated draft of an essay written by Louisa provides further indications that she had made the conscious decision to improve herself in the summer of 1824. Entitled "Female Education," it exhorts the reader to reflect on the social and moral benefits of educating the female mind. Perhaps Louisa was also reflecting on her own life and her own education:

> Female Education
>
> With what peculiar sensations does the subject of female education light upon the mind of reflection. How does the genius of all human

glory weep over the fate of her who is destined to supine ignorance. If we look around us in the world we see numbers who are susceptible of improvements nature has done her part she has blessed them with superior minds, forms and dispositions but from the grossest neglect no ray of refinement has ever lighted that mind, which is by nature as fragrant as myrtle. That mind which should have been their greatest care from childhood life has been left to grow up full of wildness extravagance & evil disposition. How unfit such a mind for enjoying the beauties of nature and of art. [H]ow unfit for enjoying the pleasures of society how exampled such a one feels surrounded by those whose imagination enlightened by education and extensive reading sparkes as the meteors of the morning. How dull and tedious must pass her hours whose mind is not enlightened even enough to give her a taste for reading, what can she enjoy. [W]hat can she do. It is no wonder that females have so long been thought almost nothing scarcely allowed to think scarcely to speak. They will ever remain unfit for society as long as their educations are so much neglected.[11]

NOTES

1. Louisa was the third of eight children born to Winifred Lane (1780–1872) and James Peleg Rogers (ca. 1775–1819).
2. Letter from C. P. R. to Louisa H. Rogers, dated July 19, 1824, manuscript collection no. 696, subseries 1.2, box 3, folder 1, Loula Kendall Rogers Papers, 1811–1954, Manuscript, Archives, and Rare Book Library (MARBL), Emory University, Atlanta, Georgia (hereafter cited as MARBL).
3. Louisa H. Rogers Album, manuscript collection no. 696, series 4, box 30, folder 12, Loula Kendall Rogers Papers, 1811–1954, MARBL.
4. "Farewell to Ashevill," dated October 13, 1824, Louisa H. Rogers Album, manuscript collection no. 696, series 4, box 30, folder 12, Loula Kendall Rogers Papers, 1811–1954, MARBL.
5. Letter from Louisa Rogers, August 24, 1825, manuscript collection no. 696, subseries 1.2, box 3, folder 2, Loula Kendall Rogers Papers, 1811–1954, MARBL.
6. Louisa H. Rogers copy book, 1825, manuscript collection no. 696, subseries 4, box 30, folder 13, Loula Kendall Rogers Papers, 1811–1954, MARBL.
7. Undated invitations, manuscript collection no. 696, subseries 1.2, box 3, folder 1, Loula Kendall Rogers Papers, 1811–1954, MARBL. These appear to date between 1817 and 1821.

8. Letter from C. P. R. to Louisa H. Rogers, dated July 19, 1824, manuscript collection no. 696, subseries 1.2, box 3, folder 1, Loula Kendall Rogers Papers, 1811–1954, MARBL.
9. The sampler descended in the family until the present owner acquired it.
10. Letter, September 26, 1826, manuscript collection no. 696, subseries 1.2, box 3, folder 1, Loula Kendall Rogers Papers, 1811–1954, MARBL; and undated poem by "Orange," Louisa H. Rogers Album, manuscript collection no. 696, series 4, box 30, folder 12, Loula Kendall Rogers Papers, 1811–1954, MARBL. Louisa's second husband, whom she married in 1836, was Dr. David Lane Kendall.
11. Louisa H. Rogers Album, manuscript collection no. 696, series 4, box 30, folder 18, Loula Kendall Rogers Papers, 1811–1954, MARBL.

Eliza WILSON

Our days alas our mortal days
Are short and wretched too;
Evil and few, the Patriarch says,
And well the Patriarch knew.

Tis but at best a narrow bound
That heaven alots to man,
Sins and pains run through the round
Of three score years & ten.

In 1815, at the age of twenty, Eliza Wilson took the unusual step of embroidering a simple marking sampler with alphabets, numerals, and two poems. She adapted the two-stanza poem above, beginning "Our days alas our mortal days," from Isaac Watts's four-verse Hymn 39, "The Shortness and Misery of Life." In the first verse, the "Patriarch" refers to the Old Testament figure Jacob, who, when asked his age by an unidentified Pharaoh, replied that he was 130, but that his ancestors had lived much longer (Genesis 47:9). The line "Of three score years & ten" refers to the span of a man's life as expressed in Psalm 90:10.

Eliza recorded only the first two lines of a second poem: "Eliza Willson is my name / single is my life &c." Her addition of the ampersand suggests that viewers would recognize the rest of the poem. In fact, the lines begin a then-popular four-line rhyme with many variations, all of which survive only

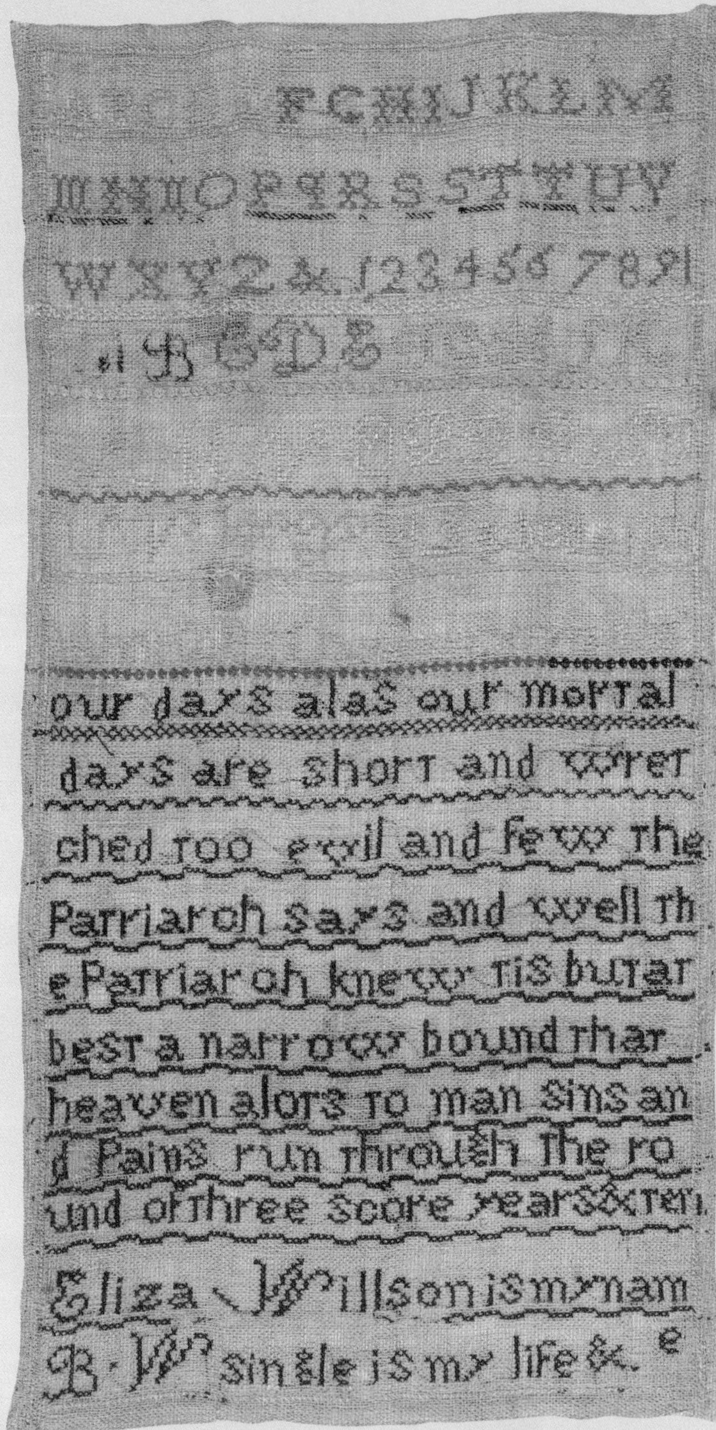

FGHIJKLM

MNNOPPRSSTTUV

WXYZ& 123456789

ABCDE

our days alas our mortal
days are short and wret
ched too evil and few the
Patriarch says and well th
e Patriarch knew tis but at
best a narrow bound that
heaven alows to man sins an
d Pains run through the ro
und of three score years & ten.

Eliza Willson is my nam
B W single is my life &. e

in manuscript form. One example reads: "[Name] is my name and single is my life and happy will that young miss be that gets to be my wife."[1]

The sixth of ten children (and youngest of three girls) born to John Wilson (1765–1847) and Mary Robertson Wilson (1765–1826) in what was then Warren County, Eliza—or Elizabeth—never married.[2] So it is perhaps no coincidence that she fixed on the themes of age and marriage, given her own age at the time she completed her sampler. Living with her parents in 1815, she had seen two older brothers and a sister marry; within four years, another brother and sister would set up separate households. Whether by choice or lack of other prospects, after her mother's passing, in 1826, Elizabeth likely cared for her father until his death. His will, dated April 4, 1846, reflects this devotion. She probably was gifted the family's home and its contents before the will's execution. The will itself stipulated that Elizabeth was to receive five bondspersons, and "all my cleared land lying in the county of Columbia on the west side of the Todd branch to cultivate and also the privilege of timber on my wood land lying on the west side of said Todd branch."[3]

. . . Eliza—or Elizabeth—never married. So it is perhaps no coincidence that she fixed on the themes of age and marriage, given her own age at the time she completed her sampler.

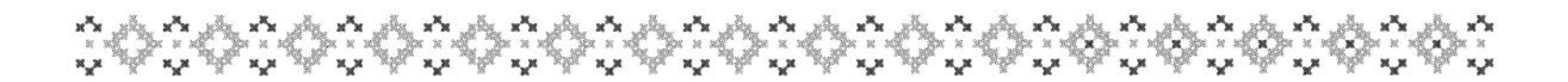

According to the 1850 federal census, Elizabeth (listed as Betsy) was a planter with real estate worth $2,000. She owned milk cows, sheep, and swine; the plantation's chief products were corn, vegetables, and butter.[4] Ten years later her plantation was valued at $1,500, but her personal property, primarily enslaved workers, was worth $8,700.[5]

Embroidered sampler by Eliza (Elizabeth) Wilson (1795–1867), dated 1815. Worker's residence: Warren County. Two-ply twisted silk thread on balanced plain weave linen. Stitches: counted cross over 2 x 2 threads. 20 1/4 x 10 1/2 inches. The Miller Collection

In the last years of her life, Elizabeth, by her own admission, was "feeble in health" although of "sound and composing Mind."[6] At the end, a Mrs. Watson nursed her, and a John C. Smith made her coffin. Among the textile-related items listed in her estate inventory are sheep shears, wool, a spinning wheel, one lot of cotton and a reel, blankets and bedding, two "Coverlids," one "fine quilt," and three carpets.[7] The sampler was not itemized. In Elizabeth's will, however, is a bequest to her sister Sarah (Sarah Wilson Scott, 1788–1875): "the Bureau with Nine drawers with their Contents." This is perhaps the same piece of furniture listed in her inventory as "1 Beaureau $15.00." The sampler descended from Sarah to Sarah's son, Adam Scott, then to Adam's son, Thomas, and finally to Thomas's daughter, Blossie Scott. It is tempting to speculate that among the contents of that nine-drawer "Beaureau" was Elizabeth's sampler.

Portraits of Mary Roberson Wilson and John Wilson, unidentified artist, ca. 1815, Warren County, Georgia. The Miller Collection.

NOTES

1. More than half a dozen nineteenth-century examples of this rhyme are recorded on the Internet; the sources include inscriptions in family bibles, a dictionary, and an arithmetic book. See, for example, the inscription by Nathaniel Dudley in Melinda Lukei, comp., *Princess Anne County, Virginia, Bible Records, Volumes 1–3*, (Virginia Beach: M.J. Lukei, n.d.), www.archive.org/details/princessannecoun13luke.
2. Much of what is known about Elizabeth Wilson's life and that of her immediate family was gleaned from unpublished sources. I am indebted to Dale Couch for providing photocopies of information from a family bible and legal documents pertaining to Elizabeth Wilson and her father, John, housed at the Georgia Archives.
3. John Wilson, will dated April 4, 1846, Warren County Wills, courtesy Dale Couch.
4. Betsy Wilson, 1850 Federal Census Non-Population Schedule 1850, Columbia County, Georgia, Ancestry.com.
5. Betsy Wilson, 1860 United States Federal Census, District 9, Columbia County, Georgia, Ancestry.com.
6. Elizabeth Wilson, will dated February 9, 1860, box 22, Columbia County Loose Estates, Georgia Archives, courtesy of Dale Couch.
7. "List of Appraisment of Miss Elizabeth Wilson Est. this Nov. 26th 1867," box 22, Columbia County Loose Estates, Georgia Archives, courtesy of Dale Couch.

No. 18

Mary Trotter HARDAWAY

Mary Trotter Hardaway was a scion of a wealthy family established in Warren County, Georgia, in the early 1800s. In 1802, Mary's father, George Hardaway (1781–1858), had set out for Warren from Dinwiddie County, Virginia. He was young and single, with money in his pocket from an inheritance and possible apprenticeship freedom dues.[1] Parentless, George may have intended to reconnect with his much older stepbrother John Hardaway (ca. 1760–1818) who had moved from Virginia to Warren County in about 1795.[2] George eventually reunited with John, who made George the administrator of his estate in 1817.[3]

In October of 1804, George married Sarah Cody (1789–1874), who was born in Warren County. Sarah's father, Edmund (1754–1832), a Virginia native and Revolutionary War veteran, and mother, Catherine Donelson (b. 1758 in North Carolina), had settled in Warren County by 1794. George likely met Sarah because his property adjoined that of his future father-in-law. The Hardaways began their married life with two hundred acres of land (possibly provided by John) and one enslaved worker.[4] By the time Mary—their eighth child—was five years old, George had added significantly to his plantation holdings and increased his bonded labor to twenty-four souls.[5]

Mary stated in stitches that she completed her sampler in 1832, when she was six. This would have been before her birthday on July 15. The embroidered patterns on her work are sophisticated and colorful, executed in surface embroidery as well as counted thread techniques. Surface embroidery, seen

---

Embroidered sampler by Mary Trotter Hardaway (1825–1912), dated 1832.
Worker's residence: Warren County. Two-ply twisted silk thread on balanced plain weave linen; top and bottom edges are selvages; right and left edges turned under twice and hemmed.
Stitches: counted cross over 2 x 2 threads; queen over 4 x 4 threads; square eyelet over 4 x 4 threads; surface split, surface satin, surface chain; surface outline, French knots. 17 5/8 x 12 1/2 inches.
Collection of Roger and Cindy Bregenzer

1234
Mary J Hardaway

in the floral sprays at the bottom of Mary's work, is an unusual feature on samplers worked in the coastal southern states and may indicate that Mary's teacher was from the North.

The embroidered patterns on her work are sophisticated and colorful, executed in surface embroidery as well as counted thread techniques.

In 1846, Mary wed Francis Meriwether Reese (1822–1892), of Monticello, Jasper County. The couple moved to Alabama before 1860 and eventually settled in Auburn. In 1903, a family historian published a sketch of Mary, who was then about seventy-eight years old:

> [She is] a handsome brunette, and possessed of considerable wealth. She is famous for her hospitalities and varied accomplishments, her home is an attractive resort for her relatives and friends. Her unassuming simplicity of manner, and cheerful disposition render her a delightful companion. She is a lovely Christian character, a zealous member of the Baptist Church. For forty-six years she lived most happily with her husband, and such was the force of her character, she made herself felt in shaping and ennobling his life, for when a young man he was much inclined to be wild, and easily led into temptations.[6]

After Mary's death, in 1912, her sampler passed to her only surviving child, Mary Meriwether Reese Frazer, and descended in the family until the late twentieth century.

NOTES

1. James Trotter Sr., will, n.d., Brunswick County, Virginia, order book 2, 482; www.genealogy.com/ftm/t/r/o/Gary-K-Trotter/GENE4-0001.html. Legacy from maternal grandfather, James Trotter, who died in Brunswick County, Virginia, in 1783. There is a family tradition of George's apprenticeship to a hatter in Dinwiddie County; see Sarah Donelson Hubert, *Thomas Hardaway of Chesterfield County, Virginia, and His Descendants* (Richmond, VA: Whittet and Shepperson, 1906), 20.
2. Hubert, 12.
3. George Hardaway, for the estate of John Hardaway, Captain Rowlands District, Warren County, Georgia, property tax 1817, Georgia, Property Tax Digests, 1793–1892, Ancestry.com (hereafter cited as Georgia Property Tax Digests).
4. George Hardaway, Captain David Neal District, Georgia Property Tax Digests.
5. George Hardaway, Captain Rowlands District, Georgia Property Tax Digests.
6. Mary E. Reese, *A Genealogy of the Reese Family in Wales and America* (Richmond, VA: Whittet and Shepperson, 1903), 192.

No. 19

Mary SANSOM

Mary Wills Sansom's squarish sampler, with its panel of fletching-like trees, might have been overlooked or miscatalogued in the twentieth century were it not for the fact that her husband's sister married James K. Polk, eleventh president of the United States.

Mary was the sixth of seven children born in Washington, Wilkes County, to William Sansom (ca. 1752–1818) and Elizabeth Darcy Napier Sansom (1775–1847). During the Revolutionary War, William had served as a sergeant in the 7th Virginia Regiment, sustaining a gunshot wound in his left arm.[1] Sometime between 1785 and 1789, as a single man, he set out for Georgia. Like countless others from Virginia and North Carolina, he took advantage of the offer of headright settlement on lands that had been ceded by the Creek and Cherokee nations to the colony of Georgia in 1773.[2] By 1790, about one third of Georgia's population called Wilkes County home.[3]

In Washington, William met and, in 1790, married Elizabeth Napier. Elizabeth's father, Richard (1747–1823), had received land in Wilkes County for his military service as a colonel in the Virginia militia. (In the 1810s, Richard would leave Georgia for larger stakes in Dickson County, Tennessee.)

The Sansom family prospered almost immediately. William was active as a justice of the peace by 1791 and served as a judge for the Inferior Court of Wilkes County.[4] Although he acquired multiple tracts of land in the western part of the county, the Sansoms lived in town, enjoying a house and lot with a

---

Embroidered sampler by Mary (Polley) Wills Sansom (1800–1821), dated 1812. Worker's residence: Washington, Wilkes County. Two-ply silk thread on balanced plain weave linen. 16 1/2 x 15 1/2 inches. James K. Polk Home and Museum, Columbia, Tennessee

dairy on the property.[5] Mary was born in 1800; at some time in her youth or teen years, she was given a personal slave.[6]

Mary was twelve when she completed her sampler. She may have attended the local Washington Academy, a trustee-administered, coeducational institution founded in 1786. No school records survive from 1812, the year on Mary's embroidery, but a newspaper advertisement for 1814 noted that a Mrs. Bowen was in charge of the female division of the academy, where "Needle work of every kind [is] taught, plain flowering and fancy work, embroidery and fillagree."[7]

No school records survive from 1812, the year on Mary's embroidery, but a newspaper advertisement for 1814 noted that a Mrs. Bowen was in charge of the female division of the academy . . .

The 1810s were a decade of change in the Sansom household. Mary's older sister Ann (1793–1824) married in 1811. Eldest brother, Dorrell (1791–1834), headed to Williamson County, Tennessee, before 1815; brother Richard (1798–1828) was in Dickson, Tennessee, before 1820. William, the patriarch, died in 1818.

Mary herself was in Williamson County, Tennessee, by 1820. On December 20 of that year she married Anderson Childress (1799–1837), a successful lawyer from Murfreesboro, Tennessee. The following year the couple was living in Franklin; on September 3, Mary gave birth to their only child, also named Mary. It may have been a difficult delivery, and perhaps there were complications. The couple and their new daughter soon relocated to Murfreesboro to be near Anderson's family. Mary Wills Sansom Childress died there on October 22. Six years later, in 1827, Anderson died tragically when he was thrown from his horse.

Orphaned daughter Mary was eighteen when, in 1840, she wed Robert Jetton (b. ca. 1820), a planter with sizable personal and estate properties. Three boys were born to the couple. In April 1847, Mary had a daughter, Sarah (or Sally) Polk Jetton (1847–1924). Three months later, echoing her mother's distressing end, Mary died, probably of childbirth complications. Robert took charge of the boys. By 1850, however, Sarah was under the guardianship of her great aunt, Sarah Childress Polk, Anderson Childress's sister and now widow of President James K. Polk.[8]

NOTES

1. Elizabeth D. Sansom, pension W.311, Revolutionary War Pension and Bounty-Land Warrant Application Files, National Archives and Records Administration (NARA), Fold3.com.
2. For transcriptions of primary sources relating to ceded lands in Georgia, see Robert Scott Davis Jr., comp., *The Wilkes County Papers, 1773–1833* (Easley, SC: Southern Historical Press, 1979).
3. Between 1790 and 1825 six new counties were carved out of Wilkes: Elbert (1790), Oglethorpe (1793), Warren (1793), Lincoln (1796), Madison (1811), and Taliaferro (1825).
4. Michal Martin Farmer, *Wilkes County Georgia, Deed Books A – W, 1784–1806* (Dallas, TX: Farmer Genealogy Co., 1996).
5. Ibid., 704 and 762. After William's death, his executors sold the house and lot and other property to the bank for $4,000; see Grace Gillam Davidson, comp., *Early Records of Georgia: Wilkes County* (1933; repr., Vidalia, GA: Rev. Silas Emmett Lucas Jr., 1968), 188.
6. Elizabeth D. Sansom, pension W.311, Revolutionary War Pension and Bounty-Land Warrant Application Files, NARA, Fold3.com.
7. *Georgia Argus* (Milledgeville, GA), August 10, 1814.
8. Sarah Polk, 1850 and 1860 United States Federal Censuses, Nashville, Davidson, Tennessee, Ancestry.com. When she was fourteen, Sarah Childress (1803–1891) completed a silk embroidery at the Moravian-run Salem Female Academy in Salem, North Carolina. This needlework is at the James K. Polk Home as well. See "Tennesse Sampler Survey: Exhibition: 1818 Sarah Childress," Tennessee Sampler Survey, www.tennesseesamplers.com.

No. 20

Eliza BLUNT

In books or works or healthful play
Let my first years be past
That I may give for ev'ry day
Some good account at last

The Architecture

Architectural embroideries are uncommon in Georgia needlework, and only five are known, including Eliza Blunt's sampler. Four of these are composed of archetypal Georgian houses that may or may not be stitched representations of specific structures. Eliza's needlework probably shows the original Eatonton Academy. The school was founded in 1807, and its first building was erected shortly thereafter, but a more commodious building was constructed some time between 1816 and 1817. Eatonton was first called Union Academy and founded in part by Alonzo Church, the notable educator later associated with the University of Georgia (then Franklin College). The first rector was a visiting young northerner, William H. Seward, who went on to be Secretary of State under President Lincoln.[1] The Georgia legislature passed an act in 1816: "To incorporate Eatonton academy in the county of Putnam, and to invest the funds of Union Academy in said county in the Trustees of Eatonton academy."[2] The first director of the female department, hired in the early summer of 1817 for the start of classes in July, was a Miss J. Kingsbury, from Boston.[3]

Embroidered sampler by Eliza S. Blunt (1806 or 1811–ca. 1854), ca. 1815–25. Worker's residence: Putnam County. Worked at: attributed to Eatonton Academy, Eatonton, Putnam County. Two-ply twisted silk thread on balanced plain weave linen; edges turned under and hemmed. Stitches: counted cross over 2 x 2 threads; queen over 4 x 4 threads; square eyelet over 4 x 4 threads; irish. 16 3/4 x 17 inches (framed). Collection of Roger and Cindy Bregenzer (detail above)

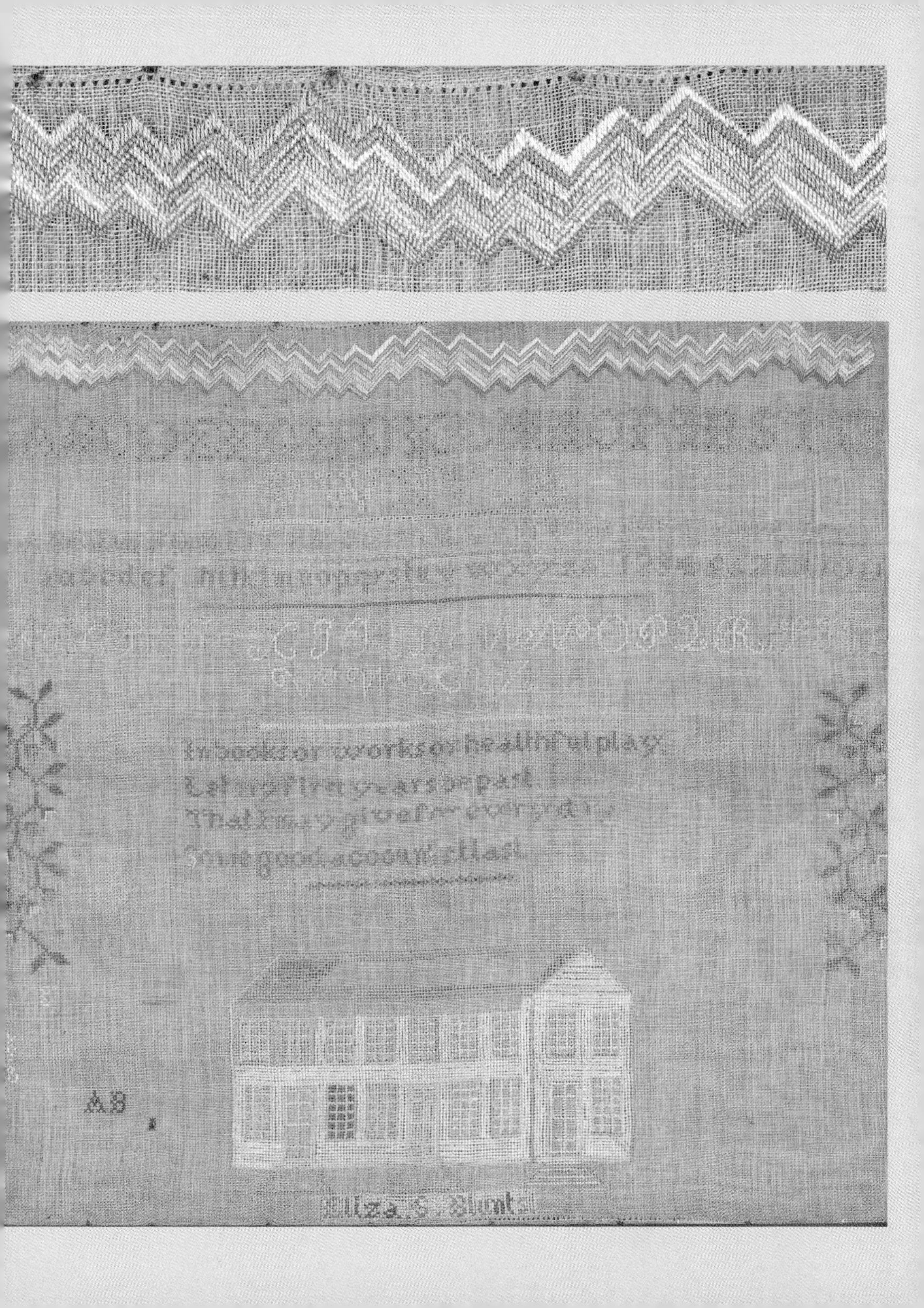
Inbooksorworksorhealthfulplay
AB
Eliza S. Blunt

Advertisements for the academy routinely referenced separate departments for males and females, and the curriculum differed dramatically. Community tradition holds that the institution was gender-segregated, and Eliza alluded to the physical separation in working two doors on her rendering of the building. Moreover, buildings with multiple front doors, especially public buildings, were common to the Georgia vernacular, and Old Union Church in Eatonton was a nearby example. Multiple front doors on the sampler almost certainly indicate that Eliza has delineated a public building.

Although the missing features are notable, there are a number of other indications that Eliza's image on the sampler represents the original Eatonton Academy building.

The embroidered building's form is typical of a widespread American vernacular known in Georgia as "plain-style plantation." Created with two rooms above two rooms and central hallways (shed rooms and piazzas were add-ons), these buildings were common among yeoman farmers and planters. The embroidered building lacks two defining southern traditions: a piazza and exterior chimneys, but this may be because Eliza never completed the sampler, as evidenced by the unfinished roof. Whether the physical academy building also did not have these elements is not known, because no visual record survives. What we do know is that, when the school was replaced in 1845, specifications for a piazza and chimneys were included in the published call for bids.[4]

Although the missing features are notable, there are a number of other indications that Eliza's image on the sampler represents the original Eatonton

Academy building. For example, the generous presence of windows in the depicted building is consistent with Georgia's architectural norms. The 1845 specifications called for windows with eighteen panes, which would have provided the ample light needed for teaching schoolchildren and may have been in keeping with the original building. Another unusual feature in the needlework is the side gable entrance, which would seem to represent a distinctive feature on a real building. Additionally, descending steps displayed in the embroidery suggest that there was a raised foundation under the building. This type of foundation might show up in any illustration of a Georgian-style house, but, in this image, its inclusion hints at local building practices—raised foundations were common to almost all house types south of Pennsylvania at the time of this needlework. Because the building displays large windows and multiple entrances, it is likely that this image is, at the very least, a partially descriptive representation of the Eatonton Academy. Moreover, school representations are known to have been used in some girlhood embroidery.[5] Eliza's sampler is likely the sole example of Georgia needlework depicting a real school.

Chesapeake Cultural Transference

A formative dimension of the Georgia Piedmont in Eliza's time was the influence of Chesapeake culture from Virginia, which conditioned the new region's society. Although the edifice Eliza depicted gives hints of Chesapeake building features, it is another part of her sampler that creates a specific style linked to Virginia: the distinctive flame-pattern band at the top of the sampler in irish stitch (a series of vertical stitches worked in a stair pattern).[6] Dating to at least the sixteenth century in Europe, this pattern was especially popular with Virginia sampler makers. Its appearance in Eliza's embroidery is significant material evidence of this cultural transfer from older, European-settled parts of the South to the freshly settled Georgia frontier. This irish stitch motif is one of the most distinctive attributes of the embroidered works of eastern Virginia.[7] Some Virginia schoolteachers taught in Georgia, and the irish stitch motif could have been passed on to Eliza by a relative born in Virginia, a sampler that migrated from Virginia, or an instructor who came from Virginia.[8]

Early Life

Eliza is variously reported to have been born in 1806 and in 1811.[9] She was the daughter of Edmund and Mary Blunt, who came to Putnam County from Columbia County about the time of Eliza's birth. Edmund Blunt's will was recorded in 1825, but he may have died the year before.[10] Edmund Blunt bequeathed $1,500 to Eliza, a considerable sum at that time. His will also mentions his widow and Eliza's five siblings: Henry W. S. Blunt, Thomas E. Blunt, Peter Blunt, Ann Spier, and Mary Ann Louisa Blunt. Eliza married John C. Wood in Putnam County on February 16, 1840.[11]

No personal records from Eliza, such as letters or a diary, are known to exist, but evidence for her life can be distilled from the records of the males (father, husband, and brother) in her life and her sampler.[12] We may never be able to develop a biography of this young needleworker (and later mother and plantation mistress) from these sources, but perhaps we can create a metaphorical hollow-cut silhouette and regain insight into her life.

In Eliza's time, needlework was both a practical skill and a signifier of refinement. It identified Eliza's social standing, and it promoted her effectiveness as mistress of a plantation. In practical terms, she would have been trained to oversee the work and well-being of her family's enslaved servants and laborers and would have been well prepared for her eventual role as a plantation mistress in Morgan County.

The acquisition of material goods maintained nuances of class, including the stark contrasts of black and white and enslaved and free. This system permeated Eliza's life and is reflected in the personal goods purchased through her inheritance. Examples of textile-related purchases from December of 1823 found in the records of Edmund Blunt's estate include the following:

5 yards Casimere
1 Bolt of Ribbon
2 gross of buttons
1 skean of silk
4 yards of flannel
1 pair of cotton cards
1 yard of shirting
1 cotton (illegible)

Eliza's sampler is likely the sole example of Georgia needlework depicting a real school.

In 1824, four needles were purchased through the family purchased a half-yard of homespun, two hanks of floss cotton, and "1 fancy Blue Ball." These purchases suggest an emphasis on needlework activity in the home. That William Cooke (of the firm of McNeil and Cooke) was paid for the "cutting of a suit" and making of a coat for Eliza's brother Thomas Blunt suggests either that the women at home were not prepared to undertake complex sartorial projects or that Thomas Blunt could afford and preferred professional products. The latter may have been more likely because women seldom made clothes for white males who had passed the breeching age of six.

Marriage and Later Life

Why Eliza married relatively late cannot be known. Certainly, she felt no economic need to be married early. No indication is evident that she was needed at home. Her mother, though aging, had property and slaves to attend to her, and also could have lived in the prosperous households of her other children.[13] When Eliza did marry, she accepted her proposal from a man of wealth and social rank—John C. Wood, a native of North Carolina residing in neighboring Morgan County, Georgia. She became a mistress of a plantation of some forty slaves. As a woman of practical experience with her own slaves, a broad education, and a conservative religious faith to which she was apparently devoted, she was probably well prepared for her role. In 1843, she gave birth to a son, John, and in 1845, she bore a second son, Edward. Eliza died about 1854. The 1850 Federal Census Population Schedule for Morgan County shows John C. Wood owning $6,000 worth of land. The 1860 Census shows him owning $8,000 worth of land, a substantial increase. Additionally, he is recorded as having $43,000 of personal wealth. The latter figure would indicate a substantial holding of enslaved people. It is difficult to determine if this increase in wealth was due to Eliza's death, as her own wealth was likely subsumed into Wood's assets. The 1860 census also indicates that Wood remarried, to Nancy F. Wood. She is recorded as being born in Massachusetts. We can only wonder if she was as well prepared as Eliza to be a mistress of a plantation.

Religious Life

The religious verse on Eliza's sampler is the last stanza of a children's hymn entitled "Against Idleness and Mischief," first published by the English Nonconformist theologian Isaac Watts in 1720.[14] Watts was a prolific hymn writer, and his verses often appear on samplers. Its inclusion in Eliza's work underscores the importance of religion and specifically the Baptist faith in her world. Her brother Henry Blunt became the clerk of a local Baptist church congregation—Crooked Creek Baptist Church.[15] In the American Revolutionary period and following, Baptists came to Georgia in part to avoid the established Episcopal (Anglican) Church in Virginia, where Baptist preachers had been discouraged and forced to seek licenses to preach.[16]

Needlework was both a practical skill and a signifier of refinement. It identified Eliza's social standing, and it promoted her effectiveness as mistress of a plantation.

At Crooked Creek, Henry kept the church minutes, which have survived. Eliza's name occurs in the minutes beginning about 1830. By 1840, the local churches along the Ocmulgee River were embroiled in the missionary versus anti-missionary controversy. On the moderate end of this dispute were the Jesse Mercer Baptists; on the opposite end were the isolationists, who believed that foreign missions were unbiblical. Henry and family appear to have gracefully withdrawn from Crooked Creek as it developed leanings toward the radical, anti-missionary (i.e., Primitive Baptist) position. Eliza and John C. Wood were married at Old Union Church in Eatonton by its pastor, Rev. John Hillyer. Interestingly, Hillyer was a Mercer associate.

As is the case for most young women of the period, the insight that can be gained about Eliza is largely indirect. We learn about Eliza through the recorded shadows of her father, her brother, and her husband.[17] As the surviving daughter of her deceased father, his estate records shed light on her life. As the congregant of a church in which her brother recorded the minutes

As is the case for most young women of the period, the insight that can be gained about Eliza is largely indirect. We learn about Eliza through the recorded shadows of her father, her brother, and her husband.

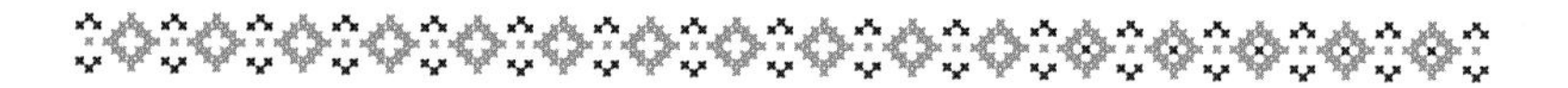

and as the wife of John Wood, a blurry profile of Eliza as an individual emerges. Unsurprisingly, we do not have an obituary or death record for her passing (ca. 1854). In some cases, even the death of a woman of property did not create estate records. Consequently, it is not her own obituary that provides our final glimpse of Eliza, but the biography of her prominent son that mentions her: "She was a devoted member of the Baptist church and a noble Christian woman."[18]

Dale L. Couch

NOTES

1. Seward was very young at the time. The scandal that he had fathered a child by an African American woman reached its high point during the Civil War when he served on Abraham Lincoln's cabinet. See E. Merton Coulter, "Seward and the South: His Career as a Georgia Schoolmaster," *Georgia Historical Quarterly* 53, no. 2 (June, 1969): 146–64.
2. *Milledgeville Georgia Journal*, September 11, 1816.
3. *Milledgeville Georgia Journal*, June 17, 1817.
4. *Milledgeville (GA) Southern Recorder*, July 21, 1846.
5. St. Joseph's Academy in Maryland was the repeated subject of girls' samplers from that school, and it is interesting that these samplers most often include a secondary building with two front doors, similar to the structure embroidered here.
6. This stitch is sometimes referred to as "flame stitch" or "bargello work."
7. For a discussion of the irish stitch motif in Virginia samplers, see Kimberly Smith Ivey, *In the Neatest Manner: The Making of the Virginia Sampler Tradition* (Williamsburg, VA: Curious Works Press and the Colonial Williamsburg Foundation, 1997), 53.
8. The *Athens (GA) Banner* for February 18, 1827, carries a repeated ad by L. and V. LaTaste assuring readers that they are southern-born teachers and natives of Virginia. The advertisement was placed to dispel rumors of abolitionists teaching in Georgia. In the *Milledgeville Georgia Journal* on Decem-

ber 3, 1817, an advertisement referring to the Eatonton Academy references a New York teacher: "To the Female Department will be added the services of a lady from New York, well recommended; she has not yet arrived but will . . . be here in due time."

9. Her age reported in the Federal Census Population Schedule of Morgan County for 1850 suggests a date of 1806. See also Southern Historical Association, *Memoirs of Georgia: Containing Historical Accounts of the State's Civil, Military, Industrial and Professional Interests, and Personal Sketches of Many of its People*, vol. 2 (Atlanta, GA: Southern Historical Association, 1895), 596. A reference to her in her son's biography in *Memoirs of Georgia* states a birth year of 1811.
10. The estate record file of Edmund Blunt contains his will, estate inventory, and various annual returns made after his death. The returns document expenditures and proceeds of the estate during its administration. All references to his estate records in this essay refer to this file, which is in Record Group 217, Loose Estate Records of Putnam County, Georgia Archives.
11. John C. Wood to Eliza S. Blunt, *Putnam County Georgia Marriage Book D, 1829–1842*, Putnam County Ordinary Court, Georgia Archives. John Hillyer, M.G., signed that he officiated their marriage on February 16, 1840.
12. The line of descent of this embroidery is not clear. The recent provenance is as follows: The present owners acquired Eliza Blunt's sampler from the author,.who acquired it from John West. West obtained the sampler from Jane Torbert Rittlemeyer. Rittlemeyer was a friend of West and had a terminal illness. She was preparing her effects for her death and had identified the sampler as material to send to a thrift store. When Rittlemeyer discovered that West liked the piece, she offered it to him in appreciation for his services in assisting her. Rittlemeyer was a native of Greensboro, Georgia. She was born in 1908 and died in 1996. She was married to John M. Rittlemeyer of Atlanta. The sampler was mounted in a frame that appears to date about 1920–40. A label that remained on the cardboard backing refers to a Greensboro business. The label appears to date 1920–40. The original sealing tape has a logo of a Goodyear store.
13. Edmund Blunt's estate held twelve slaves. The annual returns of the estate indicate that some of these slaves were rented out for income.
14. Isaac Watts, *Divine Songs for Children* (London: 1720).
15. All references regarding Crooked Creek Baptist Church were taken from a bound, mimeographed transcription of that church's record at Georgia Archives. See Francis Flournoy, *"Minutes of Crooked Creek Church, Putnam County, Georgia; Constituted 27th June 1807 by Francis Flournoy—Presbytery,"* June 27, 1807, Georgia Archives. This source is a catalogued as a published book and is in the Search Room of Georgia Archives.
16. For a discussion about the rise of Baptists in Virginia, see Rhys Isaac, *The Transformation of Virginia 1740–1790* (Chapel Hill: University of North Carolina Press, 1982).
17. Southern Historical Association, *Memoirs of Georgia*, 596. The text of that entry is as follows: "JOHN T. WOOD, farmer, Madison, Morgan Co., Ga, was born in 1841, on the farm where he now lives. He was the son of John C. and Eliza S. (Blount) Wood. The father was born in North Carolina in 1793 and came to Georgia when twenty five years old. He started for the war of 1812, but before he reached Baltimore it was over. He was a justice of the peace in Morgan county for many years, and a farmer all his life. His wife was born in Putnam county in 1811 and was the daughter of Edmund Blount. She was a devoted member of the Baptist church and a noble Christian woman. Mr John T. Wood was reared on the farm and given a good education. In 1861 he enlisted in the state militia under Col. Cowart, and later was sent to Virginia. In February, 1864, he joined Cobb's legion of cavalry and remained there until the war closed, serving as a good and loyal soldier and

brave man. In 1868 he married Rebecca L., daughter of Benjamin and Eliza (Brown) Harris. This union has been cheered by ten children, nine of whom are living: Edward H., William B., John H., Benjamin, Olander S., Anna M., Ruby L., Thomas M. and Oliver M. The deceased child was Birdie. Mr. Wood and wife are members of the Baptist church. He has been a notary public in his district for twenty years. He joined the masonic lodge when he was twenty five years old and is high in its degrees. Mr. Wood is a popular and respected citizen, and lives with his interesting family on his fine farm near Madison."

18. Ibid.

No. 21

Harriet BENTON

Harriet Benton's parents, Abba (1788–1854) and Martha (ca. 1789–1850) Benton, were North Carolinians who met and married before they settled near the town of Monticello in Jasper County, Georgia. Their marriage was recorded in Johnston County, North Carolina, in January of 1815. In May of that year, Abba collected pay for his military service in the War of 1812.[1] Perhaps this sum helped satisfy local debts or defray travel costs because the couple relocated to Georgia shortly after in the summer or early fall. Harriet was born in Jasper County on November 18, 1815.

Although Jasper County was a prime cotton-growing region and Abba did grow cotton, he concentrated on crops that he might have been more familiar with back in North Carolina—corn, oats, sweet potatoes, and legumes. Through the labor of his enslaved workers, he was also successful with livestock: cows for butter and beef, swine for meat, and a flock of sheep for wool production.[2]

Laid out as a town in 1808, Monticello was a thriving community when the Bentons arrived in the area, and the family likely took advantage of all the town had to offer, from shopping and worshipping to getting medical and legal advice. According to the 1829 *Gazetteer of the State of Georgia*, that advantage included "55 houses, 19 stores, 8 shops, 3 doctor shops, 5 law offices, a female academy, courthouse, jail and houses of worship for Baptists and Methodists."[3]

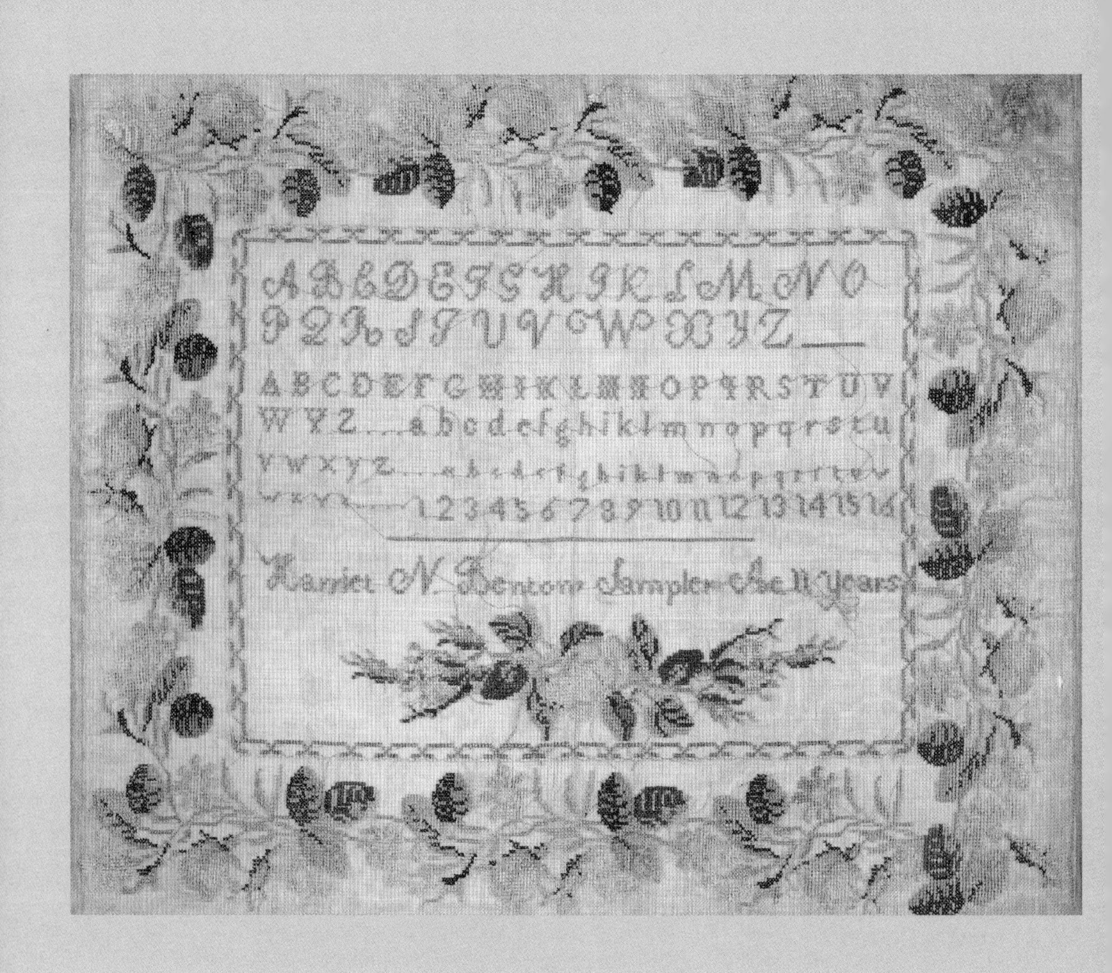

A B C D E F G H I K L M N O
P Q R S T U V W X Y Z
A B C D E F G H I K L M N O P Q R S T U V
W Y Z abcdefghiklmnopqrstu
vwxyz abcdefghiklmnopqrstv
1 2 3 4 5 6 7 8 9 10 11 12 13 14 15 16
Harriet N Benton Sampler Ae 11 Years

In about 1826, eleven-year-old Harriet completed a sampler, which features rows of stitched alphabets and numbers surrounded by an elegant, deep border of roses, open-face flowers, and foliage. Her teacher is unknown, but Harriet almost certainly received her education at nearby Monticello Female Academy. The trustee-administered academy opened in May of 1823 under the direction of a Miss Usher. A Connecticut native, Usher had taught previously at Yorkville Female Academy in South Carolina.[4] The school's newspaper advertisement for June 7 of that year argued that because Monticello was a much healthier situation than the "low . . . parts of the country," students would not be interrupted in their studies "by a long vacation to escape sickness." The tuition rates matched those of Yorkville Academy, and students could learn academic subjects such as reading, English grammar, arithmetic, composition, geography, and history. Tuition for needlework and plain sewing was one dollar per quarter. Those who were up to the challenge could take "Drawing, Painting, Filligree, Tambour and Embroidery" for ten dollars per quarter.[5] (It is notable that in the June 14, 1823, issue of the *Augusta Chronicle*, Usher's notice for Monticello Female Academy appears just above an advertisement for Yorkville Female Academy.)

Her teacher is unknown, but Harriet almost certainly received her education at nearby Monticello Female Academy.

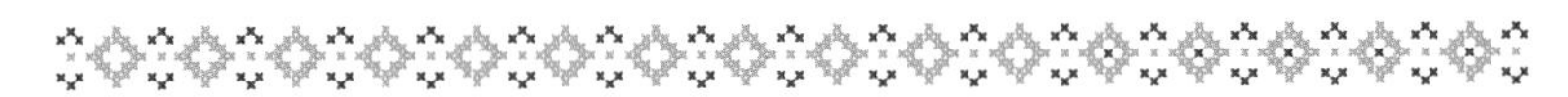

At the end of 1825, Usher's efforts were publically acknowledged by the academy's board of trustees: "Miss Usher possesses an uncommon talent for instructing young ladies, in all the useful and ornamental branches of education, usually taught at female seminaries. The Trustees feel in the duty to

Embroidered sampler by Harriet N. Benton (1815–1869), ca. 1826. Worker's residence: near Monticello, Jasper County. Two-ply twisted silk thread on balanced plain weave linen. Stitches: counted cross over 2 x 2 threads. 17 1/4 x 21 1/4 inches (framed). Collection of Judge Eugene and Christie Benton

state, that the high reputation, which the school has acquired, is to be ascribed in a great degree to the enterprising exertions of Miss Usher."[6]

Harriet was eighteen when, in January of 1834, she wed Robert Barnes (ca. 1813–1898). The couple settled on a plantation in Jasper County and raised four children. She died in 1869; her sampler passed through descendants to the current owner.

NOTES

1. Benton was in the company of Gates Militia (North Carolina) commanded by Captain Thomas Freeman, which was charged with defending the coastline. On May 7, 1815, North Carolina issued him a voucher, which he redeemed for cash, "for military service by detached militia." "Abbey Benton" is listed as a member of North Carolina's 1st Regiment, 7th Company, detached from the Gates Regiment, under Capt. Freeman in North Carolina Adjutant General's Department, *Muster Rolls, Soldiers of the War of 1812 Detached from the Militia of North Carolina 1812 and 1814* (Raleigh: North Carolina General Assembly, 1851), 7, https://archive.org/stream/musterrollsofsol00nort/musterrollsofsol00nort_djvu.txt. Abba Benton's voucher, dated May 7, 1815, is in the collection of the War of 1812 Pay Vouchers, State Archives of North Carolina, http://digital.ncdcr.gov/u?/p16062coll7,1010.
2. Abba Benton, 1850 United States Federal Census Slave and Non-Population Schedules, District 46, Jasper County, Georgia, Ancestry.com.
3. Adiel Sherwood, *Gazetteer of the State of Georgia*, 2nd ed. (Philadelphia: J. W. Martin and W. K. Boden, 1829), 138–39.
4. Documents indicate that Usher was teaching at Yorkville Female Academy in 1821 and 1822. See Patricia V. Veasey, *Virtue Leads and Grace Reveals: Embroideries and Education in Antebellum South Carolina* (Greenville, SC: Curious Works Press; Rock Hill, SC: York County Cultural and Heritage Commission, 2003), 27.
5. *Augusta (GA) Chronicle*, June 7, 1823.
6. *Georgia Journal* (Milledgeville, GA), November 14, 1825.

Family member of JOSEPH SMITH

The stitched depiction of mourning began to gain popularity in American female academies by the early 1790s. The death of George Washington, in 1799, gave further impetus to embroidered memorials, which featured interpretations of plinths, urns, weeping willow trees, wreaths, and mourners. While surviving nineteenth-century embroidered and/or painted memorials on satin-woven silk fabric are plentiful, memorials in sampler form, like this tribute to Joseph Smith (1805–1840), are uncommon.

An unknown member of the Smith family provided life, marriage, and death dates on the memorial, flanking the information with small weeping willows. The brief but elegant elegy reads: "His days are past and gone. Alas, he is no more." Completing the inscriptions are the names of the survivors: wife Nancy Ann Smith (1820–1896), son Francis Marion Smith (ca. 1837–1892), and daughter Martha Washington Smith (ca. 1839–1901).[1] The choice of children's names seems to have reflected a sense of patriotism on the part of one or both parents. The act of recording the names of family likely helped to reinforce kinship relations at a time when the Smith family experienced dynamic change.

It is not known where Joseph Smith was born, but in December 1836, he and sixteen-year-old Nancy Ann Ryals, a North Carolina native, were married in Decatur County.[2] Located in the southwest corner of Georgia, Decatur had been Creek territory until after the War of 1812, when the land was

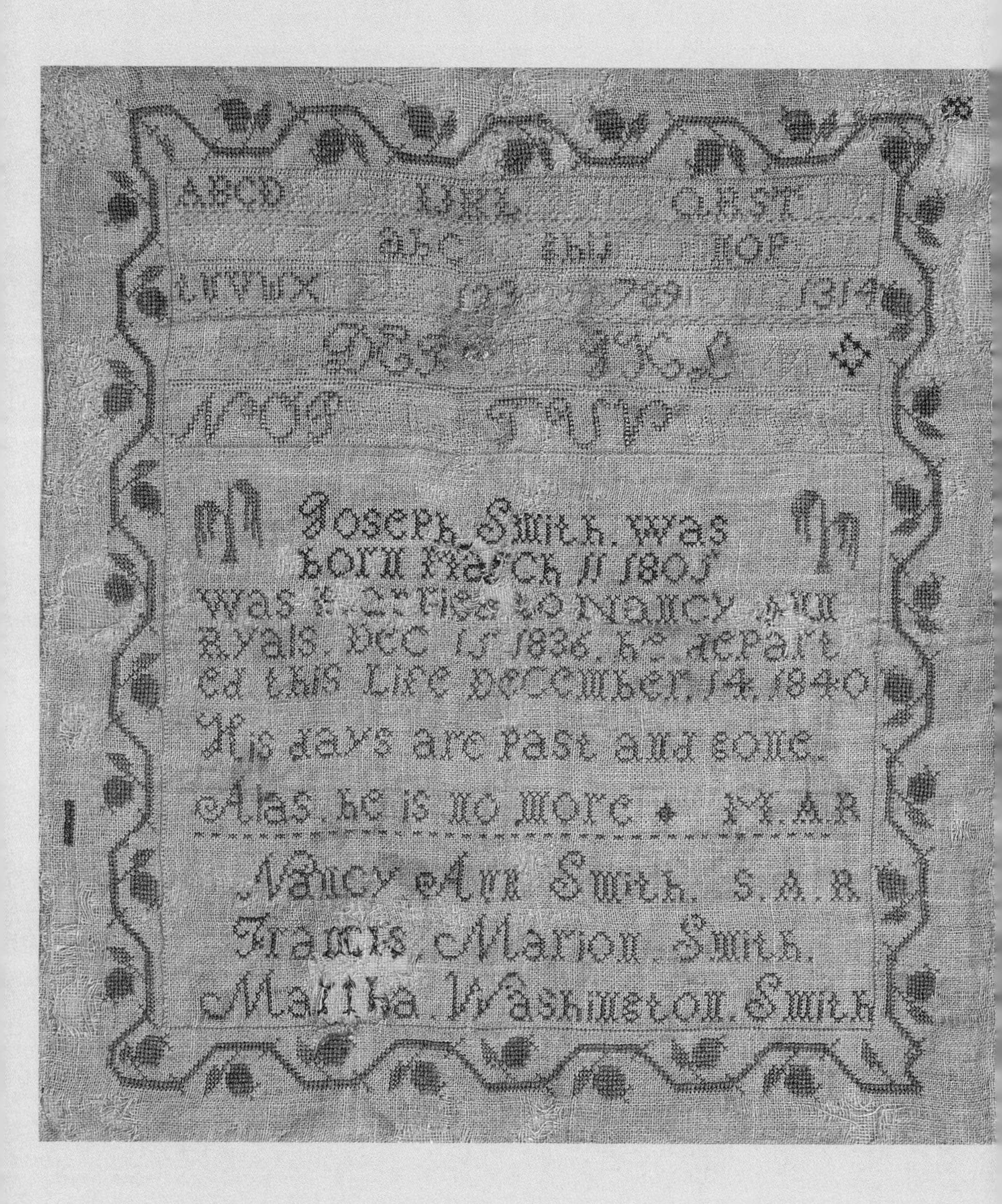
Joseph Smith. was
born March 11 1805
Ryals. Dec 15 1836. He depart
ed this life December 14. 1840
His days are past and gone.
Alas. he is no more • M.A.R
Nancy Ann Smith. S.A.R
Francis. Marion. Smith.
Martha. Washington. Smith

ceded to the federal government. By the 1830s, the county's planters were shipping cotton and wool, agricultural products, tobacco, and timber south to the Gulf of Mexico via the Flint and Apalachicola river system.[3] The 1840 federal census indicates that Joseph, who owned three slaves, was engaged in unspecified commerce.[4] That census was conducted in the summer; by mid-December, thirty-five-year-old Joseph was dead.

The act of recording the names of family likely helped to reinforce kinship relations at a time when the Smith family experienced dynamic change.

The next few years may have been uncertain ones for Nancy and her children. In 1843, Nancy remarried; her second husband, Jesse Barber Innes (1815–1855), was a carriage maker from New Jersey. The family moved south to Gadsden County, Florida, just across the border from Decatur County. By 1850, Nancy had three more children, the family owned three bondspeople, and Jesse employed three carriage makers and an apprentice, all of whom lived with the family.[5]

After Jesse's untimely death, in 1855, Nancy, Francis, and Martha returned to Decatur and settled in the county seat, Bainbridge. Francis never married and lived with his mother until his death. Martha married William Crawford Subers (1837–1906) in 1858; the sampler likely descended through their children.

NOTES

1. The stitched initials M. A. R. and S. A. R. have not been identified.
2. Decatur County, Georgia, Marriage License, Book A, 1837–1869: 7, Georgia Archives.

Embroidered sampler-style memorial to Joseph Smith by an unknown member of the Smith family, after 1840. Family's residence: Decatur County. Two-ply twisted silk thread on balanced plain weave linen. Selvages at top and bottom; left and right edges turned under twice and hemmed. Stitches: counted cross over 2 x 2 threads. 17 x 16 inches. Georgia Museum of Art, University of Georgia; Gift of Linda and David Chesnut. GMOA 2010.81

3. Selected US Federal Census Non-Population Schedules, 1850–1880, Georgia Agriculture, 1850, Decatur County, District 22, Ancestry.com; and Harry P. Owens, "Sail and Steam Vessels Serving the Apalachicola-Chattahoochee Valley," *Alabama Review* 21, no. 3 (July, 1968): 195–210.
4. Joseph Smith, 1840 United States Federal Census, Decatur County, Georgia, District 694, Ancestry.com.
5. Jesse Innes, 1850 United States Federal Census and Slave Schedules, Gadsden, Florida, District 7, Ancestry.com.

APPENDIX A: Georgia Girls Who Attended the Moravian Seminary, Bethlehem, Pennsylvania, 1791–1860

The following information is compiled from William C. Reichel and William H. Bigler, *A History of the Rise, Progress, and Present Condition of the Moravian Seminary for Young Ladies, at Bethlehem, Pa., with a Catalogue of Its Pupils, 1785–1858 . . . with a Continuation of the History and Catalogue to the Year 1870*, 2nd ed. (Philadelphia: J. B. Lippincott, 1874). The table lists students by date of enrollment.

Note: Dau. = daughter; Stepdau. = stepdaughter; Co. = county

Page	Entrance Date	Name	Birth	Relative	Residence in Georgia	Marriage/Death
334	1791	Susan Wall	July 8, 1778	Ward of William Wall	Savannah	Married William Wall, her uncle; second marriage to Nicholas Trumbull
340	1795	Sarah Hillhouse	Sept. 1784	Dau. of Daniel Hillhouse	Washington, Wilkes Co.	Married Apr. 30 1807, Andrew Shepherd
345	1799	Martha Campbell		Dau. of George Jones, MD	Savannah	

Page	Entrance Date	Name	Birth	Relative	Residence in Georgia	Marriage/Death
347	1800	Ann Maria Glenn	July 1787	Dau. of —— Glenn	Savannah	
347	1800	Sarah G. Jones	1790	Dau. of George Jones, MD	Savannah	Married Alfred Cuthbert
347	1800	Harriet C. Jones	May 1791	Dau. of George Jones, MD	Savannah	
347	1800	Ann Morrell	June 27, 1790	Dau. of John Morrell	Savannah	Married N. G. Rutherford
347	1800	Mary Ann Millen	1788	Dau. of Hon. James Jones	Savannah	Married Francis McLeod, Marietta, GA
347	1800	Ann Catherine Millen		Dau. of Hon. James Jones	Savannah	Resides with her sister
347	1800	Rebecca Pooler	1788	Dau. of John Pooler	Savannah	Died 1853
347	1800	Elvira Pooler	1790	Dau. of John Pooler	Savannah	
348	1801	Eliza Burke	1792	Ward of Joseph Clay, MD	Savannah	
348	1801	Margaret Long	Jan. 31, 17—	Dau. of Col. Nicholas Long	Washington Co.	Married Thomas Telfair, Savannah
349	1801	Rebecca Sibbald	Jan. 29, 1790	Dau. of George Sibbald	Augusta	Married —— Bethume, Fernandina, E. Florida

Page	Entrance Date	Name	Birth	Relative	Residence in Georgia	Marriage/Death
349	1801	Matilda Sibbald	May 31, 1792	Dau. of George Sibbald	Augusta	Married Charles Seton, Fernandina, E. Florida
349	1801	Eliza H. Smith	June 17, 1791	Dau. of Benajah Smith	Wilkes Co.	Married Elred Simpkins, SC
349	1801	Susan Clarke Smith	Feb. 2, 1793	Dau. of Benajah Smith	Wilkes Co.	Married —— McWhorter, MD
350	1802	Maria Holland	Oct. 19, 1790	Dau. of —— Holland	Savannah	
352	1803	Rebecca Moore	July 25, 1790	Dau. of Augustus Moore	Augusta	Married —— Dunn, MD; died 1852, in Illinois
352	1803	Prudence T. Oliver	Oct. 22, 1789	Dau. of John Oliver	Petersburg	Married Robert H. Watkins; resides (1857) at Huntsville, AL
352	1803	Sally W. Oliver	Aug. 6, 1792	Dau. of John Oliver	Petersburg	Married Dandridge Bibb, AL
352	1803	Matilda Pope	July 2, 1791	Dau. of Leroy Pope	Petersburg	
352	1803	Eliza Eleanor Thomson	Mar. 31, 1791	Dau. of Capt. Robert Thomson	Petersburg	
353	1804	Ann Watkins Douglass	Nov. 1791	Dau. of Maj. D. Douglass	Georgia	

Page	Entrance Date	Name	Birth	Relative	Residence in Georgia	Marriage/Death
355	1805	Henrietta Lillibridge	July 7, 1793	Stepdau. of Joseph Grant	Savannah	Married —— Billow, SC
356	1805	Maria Woodbridge	Jan. 23, 1793	Dau. of Thomas Woodbridge	Savannah	Married Capt. Archelaus Rea, Roxbury, MA
357	1806	Ann Glascock	Nov. 10, 1793	Dau. of Gen. T. Glascock	Augusta	Married John Malone; second marriage to Daniel Savange; died July 10, 1828
357	1806	Jane Jones		Dau. of James Jones	Burke Co.	
357	1806	Caroline M. Pooler	Dec. 25, 1792	Dau. of John Pooler	Savannah	Married John Frazer, MD; died 1849
359	1807	Mary B. Neyle	Oct. 12, 1797	Dau. of Sampson Neyle	Georgia	Married June 24, 1830, J. S. Thomas, Milledgeville, GA
359	1807	Elizabeth H. Neyle	Sept. 14, 1799	Dau. of Sampson Neyle	Georgia	Married as second wife, J. S. Thomas, Milledgeville, GA
361	1808	Sarah Noel King	Aug. 24, 1794	Dau. of Mrs. Sarah King	Savannah	
361	1808	Agnes Bacon King	May 4, 1797	Dau. of Mrs. Sarah King	Savannah	
363	1809	Claudia Harriet Tatnall		Dau. of Josiah Tatnall, Jr.	Savannah	

Page	Entrance Date	Name	Birth	Relative	Residence in Georgia	Marriage/Death
370	1814	Ann J. Davies	Dec. 28, 1800	Dau. of Judge William Davies	Savannah	Married William McIntosh; second marriage Oct. 15, 1820, to Charles J. Paine, MD, Milledgeville, GA; died Apr. 16, 1847
371	1814	Elizabeth Sarah Sturges	Apr. 23, 1802	Dau. of Oliver Sturges	Savannah	Married W. P. Hunter, Savannah, GA
371	1814	Lucretia B. Watson	Feb. 20, 1808	Dau. of Oliver Sturges	Savannah	
372	1815	Maria Doyle	1806	Dau. of Francis Doyle	Savannah	
379	1817	Ann Reynolds	Oct. 21, 1807	Dau. of R. Douglass	Savannah	Married Henry Beldon, Hartford, CT
381	1818	Jane P. Johnston	Mar. 1, 1806	Dau. of James Johnston	Savannah	Married P. M. Kollock, MD
381	1818	Louisa Johnston	Jan. 30, 1808	Dau. of James Johnston	Savannah	Married P. Houston Woodruff
381	1818	Eliza Johnston	Nov. 30, 1809	Dau. of James Johnston	Savannah	Married Edmond Molyneux Jr. British Consul
383	1819	Ann Maria Barnard		Dau. of Timothy Barnard	near Savannah	Married —— Wash, Wilmington Island, GA

Page	Entrance Date	Name	Birth	Relative	Residence in Georgia	Marriage/Death
384	1819	Elizabeth Morell		Ward of Patrick Houston	Savannah	Married Charles Dunham, New Brunswick, NJ
386	1820	Henrietta Hodgkinson	June 1809	Dau. of Mrs. John Harris	Savannah	
386	1820	Charlotte Neyle	July 3, 1806	Dau. of Sampson Neyle	Georgia	Married Horace Smith, New Haven, CT
386	1820	Emma Neyle	Dec. 3, 1809	Dau. of Sampson Neyle	Georgia	Married F. W. Heineman; died Aug. 1844
386	1820	Mary Elizabeth Ross		Dau. of Mrs. Benjamin Lamb	Bryan Co.	died Jan. 16, 1822, in the Seminary; she was buried in the Moravian graveyard
388	1821	Margaret Shick	Aug. 24, 1808		Savannah	Married R. M. Charlton
389	1822	Mary E. H. Gould	Mar. 8, 1809	Dau. of James Gould	St. Simon's Island	
391	1823	Sarah M. Aikin	Sept. 5, 1813	Stepdau. of — Brown	Savannah	Married Dunbar Morrell
391	1823	Elvira Ann Aikin	Sept. 13 1815	Stepdau. of — Brown	Savannah	Married John Hunter
392	1823	Lucy Grant	Jan. 14, 1817	Dau. of Thomas Grant	Grantsville, Greene Co.	
392	1823	Ann Elizabeth Matthews	Mar. 6, 1810	Dau. of Rev. —— Matthews	St. Simons Island	Married —— Finsley, Charleston, SC

Page	Entrance Date	Name	Birth	Relative	Residence in Georgia	Marriage/Death
393	1823	Lydia Wood	May 31, 1814	Dau. of Samuel Wood	Savannah	Married Jonathan H. Osborne, Philadelphia, PA
394	1824	Jane Gould	1815	Dau. of James Gould	St. Simons Island	Married Orville Richardson, Baltimore, MD
397	1825	Ann E. Nowlan	Dec. 5, 1808	Dau. of Col. G. G. Nowlan	Effingham Co.	Married Nov. 25, 1830, Rev. A. H. McDowell
397	1825	Margaret G. Nowlan	Sept. 18, 1812	Dau. of Col. G. G. Nowlan	Effingham Co.	Married Nov. 19, 1832, J. R. Saussey, MD, Savannah
398	1826	Elizabeth M. Charlton		Dau. of John Charleston	Willoughby, Effingham Co.	Married Dec. 27, 1836, Rev. George Wright
399	1826	Ann Georgina Nowlan		Ward of Robert Taylor	Savannah	Married Oct. 6, 1835, Daniel Remshart
401	1827	Mary Abbott			Savannah	
402	1827	Matilda W. McAllister		Dau. of George W. McAllister	Savannah	Married Thomas S. Clay, Bryan County, GA
404	1828	Caroline Jordan		Ward of James Wallace	Savannah	Married Thomas Hale; resides in Brooklyn, NY
418	1836	Emily Bugg		Dau. of Peter T. Bugg	Columbus, Muscogee Co.	

Page	Entrance Date	Name	Birth	Relative	Residence in Georgia	Marriage/Death
421	1837	Henrietta Bishop		Dau. of James B. Bishop	Augusta	Married Nov. 3, 1841, John C. Carmichael; died Apr. 11, 1854
421	1837	Mary A. Bishop		Dau. of James B. Bishop	Augusta	Married Nov. 6, 1856, William A. Alexander
422	1837	Susan W. Johnston		Dau. of J. R. Johnston	Waynesville	
425	1838	Caroline Saltmarsh		Dau. of D. Saltmarsh	Macon	
436	1844	Catharine E. Rokenbaugh		Dau. of Jacob Rokenbaugh	Darien	Married May 22, 1852, J. H. Ladson; died Mar. 22, 1853
443	1847	Louisa L. Curd		Dau. of Mrs. S. E. Curd	Macon	
474	1855	Isabella C. S. Lewis		Dau. of J. N. Lewis	Savannah	Married Dec. 1865, J. Spivey, Savannah, GA
475	1855	Eliza J. Pope		Dau. of Alexander Pope, Sen.	Washington	Married Nov. 14, 1860, —— Hull, Atlanta, GA
475	1855	Annie Pope		Dau. of Alexander Pope, Sen.	Washington	Married Com. Hunter, Washington, GA
477	1855	Mary F. Willis		Dau. of Francis Willis, MD	Savannah	

Page	Entrance Date	Name	Birth	Relative	Residence in Georgia	Marriage/Death
477	1855	Mary Jon Wragg		Dau. of John A. W. Wragg, M. D.	Savannah	Married Mar. 23, 1859, J. Bryan Bond
478	1856	Alice Connerat		Dau. of Joseph V. Connerat	Savannah	Died Mar. 10, 1859, in Philadelphia, PA
478	1856	Laleah G. Dunwody		Dau. of Rev. J. B. Dunwody	Savannah	
478	1856	Helen Ernenputsch		Dau. of Rev. W. Ernenputsch	Augusta	
479	1856	Kate M. Hartridge		Dau. of M. H. G. Hartridge	Savannah	Married 1860
481	1856	Mary L. Napier		Dau. of Leroy Napier, MD	Macon	Married —— Shellie, MD
482	1856	Julia Starr		Ward of W. C. Basinger	Savannah	
483	1857	Mary Clanton		Dau. of Turner Clanton	Augusta	Married Feb. 23, 1860, J. Pinckney Thomas, Augusta, GA
483	1857	Julia F. Clayton		Dau. of W. W. Clayton	Kingston, Cass County	Married Nov. 21, 1866, C. E. Foster Hoge, Esq., Atlanta, GA
484	1857	Anna W. Dearing		Dau. of W. E. Dearing, MD	Augusta	
484	1857	Julia Ernenputsch		Dau. of Rev. W. Ernenputsch	Augusta	Married Oct. 1867, Charles Carr

Page	Entrance Date	Name	Birth	Relative	Residence in Georgia	Marriage/Death
484	1857	Eva Eve		Dau. of William J. Eve	Augusta	Married Charles Jones, Esq., Brooklyn, NY
485	1857	Rebecca Lamar		Dau. of George Lamar	Augusta	Married 1868, A. Poullaine, Augusta, GA
488	1857	Evelyn N. West		Dau. of Charles W. West, MD	Savannah	
489	1858	Sallie Church Craig		Dau. of Lewis S. Craig	Athens	
496	1859	Fannie A. Hatch		Dau. of Milo Hatch	Augusta	
497	1859	Georgia Lawton		Dau. of R. T. Lawton	Sylvania	Married Aug. 22, 1867, Alexander E. Morgan, Nashville, TN
497	1859	Cecilia Lawton		Dau. of R. T. Lawton	Sylvania	Married Sept. 1864, Winborn W. Lawton, Charleston, SC
497	1859	Sarah Lois Monroe		Dau. of Nathan C. Monroe	Macon	Married Col. F. W. Sims, Savannah
500	1860	Kitty G. Butts		Dau. of James R. Butts	Macon	Married Aug. 15, 1867, William H. Atwood

Page	Entrance Date	Name	Birth	Relative	Residence in Georgia	Marriage/Death
502	1860	Mary Frances Hines		Ward of Richard K. Hines	Albany	Married Oct. 18, 1865 to Rev. Henry F. Hoyt, Albany, GA; died Oct. 15, 1866
502	1860	Martha C. Jennings		Dau. of William P. Jennings, MD	Albany	
504	1860	Anna Marion Richards		Dau. of Thomas Richards	Augusta	
505	1860	Clementine Strozier		Dau. of P. J. Strozier	Albany	
505	1860	Fredonia E. Strozier		Dau. of P. J. Strozier	Albany	
505	1860	Lettie H. Yonge		Dau. of George Yonge	Augusta	

APPENDIX B: Georgia Girls Who Attended Litchfield Female Academy, Litchfield, Connecticut, 1792–1833

Source: *To Ornament Their Minds: Sarah Pierce's Litchfield Female Academy, 1792-1833*, ed. Catherine Keene Fields and Lisa C. Kighlinger (Litchfield, CT: Litchfield Historical Society, 1993). The students are listed chronologically by year of attendance.

Page	Attendance	Name	Hometown in Georgia
115	1802	—— Bissell	Savannah
116	1802	—— Bourke	St. Catherine's Island
120	1802	Mary Jones Glen	Savannah
121	1802	Catherine Hunter	Savannah
128	1802	Anny Fred Simons	Georgia
122	1806–11	Eliza Johnston	Savannah
127	1808–11	Bellamy Crawford Robertson	Savannah

Page	Attendance	Name	Hometown in Georgia
127	ca. 1811	Ann Robertson	Savannah
131	1818	Eliza Wheeler	Medway
119	1819–20	Ann A. Dicks	Sunbury
123	1819–20	Ann Martha Law	Sunbury
123	1819–20	Harriet S. Law	Sunbury
123	1819–20	Maria Margaret Law	Sunbury
129	1819–21	Carolina Georgia Stevens	Sunbury
125	1820	Catheline Nichols	Augusta
130	1820–22	Mary Ann Martha Tufts	Savannah
123	1821	Catherine Barrington King	Darien
123	1821	Eliza Barrington King	Darien
130	1822	Susan Tufts	Savannah
118	1824–25	Margaret Eliza Clark	St. Marys
124	ca. 1830	Eliza Morrison	Savannah

APPENDIX C: A Sampling of Other Girlhood Embroideries Known to Have Been Worked in Georgia or Attributed to Georgia

This list of embroideries not included in the exhibition was compiled in part from samplers recorded by Ashley Callahan and Dale Couch for the Georgia Decorative Arts Survey and objects listed in museum collections.

Ball, Corinthia. n.p., n.d. Private collection.

Birtwistle, Isabella. Possibly Georgia, n.d. Augusta Museum of History, Augusta, Georgia.

Bulloch, Ann. Savannah, dated 1798. Telfair Museum of Art, Savannah, Georgia, acc. OTL4.1955.

Clay, Eliza Caroline. Bryan County, Georgia, or Medford, Massachusetts, dated August 6, 1817. Private collection. Documented by the National Society of the Colonial Dames of America in the State of Georgia, image 594.3, Henry D. Green Center for the Study of the Decorative Arts, Georgia Museum of Art, Athens.

Clay, Nancy Carolyn Bryant. Attrib. Hamilton, Harris County, or possibly Alabama, ca. 1840. Documented by the National Society of the Colonial Dames of America in the State of Georgia, image 547.3; Henry D. Green Center for the Study of the Decorative Arts, Georgia Museum of Art, Athens.

Jernigan, Martha Matilda. Powelton Academy, Hancock County, n.d. Atlanta History Center, Atlanta, Georgia, acc. 1996.206 M1.

Kissinger, Susanna. n.p., dated 1836. Oak Hill and the Martha Berry Museum, Berry College, Rome, Georgia.

McIntyre, Hannah Lawson. Thomas County, dated September 19, 1834. Embroidered memorial to Hugh McIntyre. Thomas County Historical Society.

Marshall, Eliza M. n.p., dated October 15, 1835. Documented by the National Society of the Colonial Dames of America in the State of Georgia, image 64.10, Henry D. Green Center for the Study of the Decorative Arts, Georgia Museum of Art, Athens.

Miller, Mary. Savannah, dated 1775. Described in Ethel Stanwood Bolton and Eva Johnston Coe, *American Samplers*, (1921; repr., New York: Weathervane Books, 1973), 64. Owned in 1921 by Mrs. Stanley H. Lowndes.

Mitchell, Sarah Elizabeth. n.p., dated 1810. (Sarah was the daughter of Governor David Brydie Mitchel). Owned by Mrs. Leila Lamar Sibley in 1936. Discussed in Nelle Womack Hines, *A Treasure Album of Milledgeville and Baldwin County, Georgia* (Milledgeville, GA: Press of the J. W. Burke Co., 1936), 26.

Perry, Eliza. Possibly Savannah, dated 1838. Georgia College Foundation, Old Governor's Mansion, Milledgeville, Baldwin County.

Ryan, M., and S. Waycross. Ware County, early 19th century. Documented by the National Society of the Colonial Dames of America in the State of Georgia, image 357.0, Henry D. Green Center for the Study of the Decorative Arts, Georgia Museum of Art, Athens.

Salfner, Dorthea Gnann. Ebenezer, Effingham County, dated 1782. Documented by the National Society of the Colonial Dames of America in the State of Georgia, image 580.4, Henry D. Green Center for the Study of the Decorative Arts, Georgia Museum of Art, Athens.

Smith, Tabitha Hendricks. n.p., attrib. ca. 1788. Atlanta History Center, Atlanta, Georgia, acc. 1995.108 M9.

Sproull, Eliza M. Marshall. Cartersville, Bartow County, dated October 15, 1835. Private collection.

Stokes, Harriet. Possibly Madison, Morgan County, n.d. Documented by the National Society of the Colonial Dames of America in the State of Georgia, image 175.8; Henry D. Green Center for the Study of the Decorative Arts, Georgia Museum of Art, Athens.

Thurston, Mary Jane. n.p., n.d. Gray House, Callaway Plantation, Washington, Georgia.

Unidentified maker. Possibly Savannah, after 1806. Memorial to Samuel L. Bullen. High Museum of Art, Atlanta, Georgia.

Wade, Frances. Savannah, dated 1798. Map sampler. Illustrated and described in Bolton and Coe, 83 and 219. Owned in 1921 by Miss Fannie Bleecker Seaman.

Wells, Mary Elizabeth Vallotton. Savannah, dated July 16, 1824. Private collection. Documented by the National Society of the Colonial Dames of America in the State of Georgia, image 792.0, Henry D. Green Center for the Study of the Decorative Arts, Georgia Museum of Art, Athens.

APPENDIX D: Documented Georgia Needlework Teachers and Schools, 1768–1848

This listing was compiled from Georgia newspaper advertisements. It is not exhaustive and includes only those teachers and schools—listed in alphabetical order—that offered needlework as part of the curriculum. The counties covered in this listing are: Baldwin, Camden, Chatham, Clarke, DeKalb, Elbert, Greene, Hancock, Jasper, Liberty, McIntosh, Oglethorpe, Richmond, Troup, Warren, and Wilkes. The full text transcriptions of these notices, created 2014–2015 by Kathleen Staples, are housed at the Henry D. Green Center for the Study of the Decorative Arts, Georgia Museum of Art, Athens, Georgia.

Note: County is abbreviated as Co.

Name	Location	Advertising Date(s)	Comments
Academy at Baisden Bluff	Baisden Bluff, McIntosh Co.	1820	Commissioner-administered coeducational institution; day and boarding; superintendence by Mr. and Mrs. Lindon; Mrs. Lindon in charge of boarding department and girls' education; "several branches of needlework."
Anderson, Mary	Savannah, Chatham Co.	1780	Day school; "Sewing," "Needle Work taken in."

Name	Location	Advertising Date(s)	Comments
Askew, Mary	Augusta, Richmond Co.	1811–13	Day and boarding school run by Mr. and Mrs. Askew; "fine Needle Work."
Bascom, P. E.	Savannah, Chatham Co.	1825	School at Mrs. Battey's house; "Plain and Ornamental Needle Work."
Battey, George	Savannah, Chatham Co.	1810	Intent to open day and boarding school, "Academy for Young Ladies," at subscriber's house; teachers are two unnamed young ladies; "Embroidery, Needle work on Muslin, plain Sewing."
Bedon, Elizabeth	Savannah, Chatham Co.	1769	Intent to open a boarding school; "all kinds of Needle Work."
Bissent, ——; Cowling, ——	Savannah, Chatham Co.	1810	Intent to open a day school at the home of Slauter Cowling, schoolmaster and father of —— Cowling; "marking, plain, open and flowered work, netting, &c."
Blome, Heloisa	Augusta, Richmond Co.	1821–30	Day school; "plain and ornamental Work," "Plain Work and Marking, Knitting and Fringe will be included without addition to the terms." Intent to open school with —— Carre in 1830.
Bowen, ——	Washington, Wilkes Co.	1814	See Washington Female Academy.
Briere, Jeanne Margueritte Cazaux	Savannah, Chatham Co.	1810–11	"Embroidery, Marking and Sewing," "Embroidery and Needle-Work."

Name	Location	Advertising Date(s)	Comments
Broad, L. C.	Sparta, Hancock Co.	1822	Intent to open a day school; sister Mrs. Fraser teaches music; "plain needle work and ornamental embroidery."
Brown, Sally	Savannah, Chatham Co.	1812	Intent to open day school; "marking, netting, sewing, &c."
Campbell, ——	Washington, Wilkes, Co.	1817	Intent to open school; "Embroidery, Map-work, Tambour, and various other branches of useful and Ornamental Needle-work."
Canuet, L. F.	Savannah, Chatham Co.	1815–16	Boarding school; "plain sewing and embroidery."
Cantor, ——	Savannah, Chatham Co.	1806	Day and boarding school; "marking and plain needle work."
Carr, ——	Near Bath, Richmond Co.	1814	Teacher at Mount Enon Academy; "complete Needle Work."
Carre, ——	Augusta, Richmond, Co.	1830	See Blome, Heloisa.
Cleary, ——	Augusta, Richmond Co.	1827	Coeducational day school operated by Mr. and Mrs. Cleary; "Marking, Plain and Ornamental Needle-work."
Collier, Cloe C.	Greensboro, Greene Co.	1811–16	Day and boarding school; "several kinds of Needle Work, Embroidery." Collier opened a milinary shop in Greensboro in December 1816.
Copp, ——	Milledgeville, Baldwin Co.	1788	Boarding school; "coarse and fine needlework, Shading, Tambour &c."

Name	Location	Advertising Date(s)	Comments
Cosgreve, ——	Savannah, Chatham Co.	1768	First Georgia teacher notice to include needlework; husband James Cosgreve offered educational classes for adults; "Mrs. Cosgreve would undertake to teach young Ladies to sew and read."
Coulter, ——	Augusta, Richmond Co.	1817	Intent to open day school at residence; "all kinds of Needle Work."
Courtnay, Lydia Smith (1769–1852)	Savannah, Chatham Co.	1804	Born in Newburyport, MA; married Edward Courtenay (1771–1807) of Ireland in Charleston, SC, 1794; day and boarding school; "plain sewing and a variety of other kinds of needle work."
Depass, ——	Savannah, Chatham Co.	1820	Seminary at her residence; "Embroidery, Needle, Rug & Ribbon work, Ten[t] stich, Marking, & Plain Sewing."
——	Augusta, Richmond Co.	1825	"Plain and ornamental work, rug and ten[t] stitch Embroidery."
Desmessteaux, Louisa	Savannah, Chatham Co.	1794	Day and boarding school; "all kinds of needlework, Tambour, and Embroidery," "She has followed this business many years in Jamaica," "Samples of Needlework done by her scholars can be shown to any person desirous of seeing them."
Dixon, Mary	Near Bath and Augusta, Richmond, Co.	1813	Teacher at Mount Enon Academy; "Needle-work, embroidery."

Name	Location	Advertising Date(s)	Comments
——	——	1815	Taught with Miss Miller at Richmond Academy; "plain Needle Work and Embroidery."
Douglass, ——	Washington, Wilkes Co.	1818	See Washington Female Academy.
Dugas, ——	Washington, Wilkes Co.	1806	Day and boarding school; "needlework."
——	Augusta, Richmond Co.	1809–10	"The different kinds of embroidery."
Eirick, Ruth (1754–1827)	Savannah, Chatham Co.	1787	Born in Ireland, married Alexander Eirick; widowed in 1793 and married John Armour, Savannah mason; intent to open a day school at residence; "a Variety of Needlework."
Eudisco Academy	Ruckersville, Elbert Co.	1820	Trustee-administered boarding institution under the superintendence of Miss Sarah Raymond, from Connecticut; experienced teacher; "Embroidery." See also Female Academy, Warrenton.
Female Academy, Warrenton	Warrenton, Warren Co.	1823–24	Trustee-run day and boarding school under superintendence of Sarah D. Raymond; "Embroidery."
Finley, Esther Flynt Caldwell	Bethlehem, Oglethorpe Co.	1818	From New Jersey; day and boarding school; "Needle Work."
Fleming, Mary	Augusta, Richmond Co.	1792	Intent to open a day school; "sewing, marking & embroidery."

Name	Location	Advertising Date(s)	Comments
Franklin, Mary	Milledgeville, Baldwin Co.	1809	Likely a day school; "Needle-work, plain and ornamental."
Garrety, Mary	Savannah, Chatham Co.	1775	Day school; "most Kinds of Needle-work."
Garvin, Sarah Few (1771–1855)	Augusta, Richmond Co.	1803–11	Teaching with husband, Rev. John Garvin; "different branches of Needle-work."
——	——	1819	As a widow, intent to open a boarding seminary with —— Godfrey, late from London, via New York; "Plain and Ornamental Needle Work."
Gerard, ——	Savannah, Chatham Co.	1846	From New York; "Fancy Work."
Gibbs, ——	Darien, McIntosh Co.	1818	Intent to open day school; "school-room will be close and warm"; "Needlework."
Grace, ——	Augusta, Richmond Co.	1815	Wife of Patrick H. Grace; taught needlework and embroidery in Charleston, SC, at Mrs. A. M. Talvande's school before settling in Augusta; "An assistant is also engaged to attend particularly to plain and fancy Needle-Work and Embroidery."
Green, ——	Savannah, Chatham Co.	1804–7	Fifteen years experience teaching; "Plain work &c. Embroidery, Tambour"; "muslin work"; in 1807 an assistant was employed to teach needlework.

Name	Location	Advertising Date(s)	Comments
Guerineau, ——	Augusta, Richmond Co.	1825–28	Day and boarding school; "long experience in teaching the 'young ladies'"; "Plain and Ornamental Needlework."
Hicks, Judith (Mrs. F. D.)	Greene Co.	1817	School at her residence; employs assistants; "needle work."
——	Mount Airy, Richmond Co.	1822	Day and boarding school fourteen miles north of Augusta; "embroidery."
Hueston, ——	Savannah, Chatham Co.	1803–4	From Charleston; day and boarding school; "all sorts of Needle Work, Tambour, Embroidery and Straw Works, Filigree, Artificial Flowers, with many other fancy works."
Hutchison, Susan Davis (Nye)	Augusta, Richmond Co.	1825–30	Day school; "Lace and Point Work, according to the most approved methods now practiced in New York, and in Scotland." See Nye, Susan Davis.
Hynes, ——	Savannah, Chatham Co.	1809	Likely a day school; "plain Sewing, Marking."
Jacobs, ——	Savannah, Chatham Co.	1800	Coeducational day school; "Needlework in its various branches."

Name	Location	Advertising Date(s)	Comments
Jones, M.	Augusta, Richmond Co.	1801–3	Lately from Charleston, SC; day and boarding school; "needle work in the most approved and fashionable manner, tambour," "all kinds of Needle Work, plain and flourishing; Embroidery, working and knotting counterpanes and toilets, which will be laid off in the most elegant manner; Tambour."
Jourdan, Mary E.	LaGrange, Troup Co.	1848	Teacher at LaGrange Female Seminary, which in 1848 had almost one hundred students from Georgia, Carolina, Florida, and Alabama; "Needle-Work, Embroidery."
Jull, ——	Augusta, Richmond Co.	1821–22	Day school; "Mrs. J. has also engaged a Lady to teach needle Work."
Ker, Rhoda (Hatcher) Hayes (b. ca. 1771)	Augusta, Richmond Co.	1801–3	Teacher part-time in her husband's school; "plain work, marking, embroidery, &c."
——	Savannah, Chatham Co.	1821–25	Day school with boarding offered beginning in 1822; "Plain and Ornamental Needle work, Tambour, &c."; "elegant embroidery, on lace or muslin, to any pattern."
Kingsmore, ——	Savannah, Chatham Co.	1826	Day and boarding school at residence; "various kinds of fancy work."
Lachicotte, ——	Savannah, Chatham Co.	1835	Intent to open day school at her residence; "Fancy work of various kinds."

Name	Location	Advertising Date(s)	Comments
LaTaste, Anna M. (Rockwell) (ca. 1815–1856)	Augusta, Richmond Co.	1846	New York native; day school called Augusta Female Academy; "Embroidery on Chenille, Silk, Worsted and Beads, &c."
Lewis, Helen	Savannah, Chatham Co.	1824–30	Coeducational day school; "Marking, Plain and Ornamental Needle Work."
Limbert, Catherine White (1781–1865)	Savannah, Chatham Co.	1818–25	Began teaching after death of husband William, Savannah merchant, and ceased upon marriage to Anson Hayden, Savannah dentist; "Embroidery, and other fancy needle work; plain Sewing, Marking, &c."
McCord, ——	Augusta, Richmond Co.	1847	Intent to open day school at her residence; "all manner of fancy work."
McLean, ——	Augusta, Richmond Co.	1807	Intent to open a day school; "Needle-Work."
McMillan, ——	Augusta, Richmond Co.	1813	Day and boarding school; "marking, plain and open Needle-Work, Knitting, and working a variety of fashionable and fancied Net-Works."
Miller, ——	Augusta, Richmond Co.	1815	Teacher with Mrs. Mary Dixon at Richmond Academy; "plain Needle Work and Embroidery."
Moise, H. L.	Augusta, Richmond Co.	1831–32	Day and boarding school; "Plain and Ornamental Needle Work."
Mount Enon Academy	Near Bath, Richmond, Co.	1813–14	See Carr, ——; Dixon, Mary; Miller, ——; Smith, Antoinetta.

Name	Location	Advertising Date(s)	Comments
Mount Zion Academy	Mount Zion, Hancock Co.	1818	Presbyterian coeducational school run by Nathan S. S. Beman, from Maine; Mrs. Beeman taught needlework in 1814; separate female school in 1818 under the direction of Harriet Stebbins, from New York, who taught previously at Powelton Academy, also in Hancock Co.
Monticello Female Academy	Monticello, Jasper Co.	1823–25	—— Usher, teacher, from Connecticut, taught previously at Yorkville Female Academy, SC; "Needle Work and Plain Sewing," "Filligree, Tambour and Embroidery."
Mullryne, ——	Savannah, Chatham Co.	1810	Intent to open school; "different kinds of Needle Work," "Ladies Dresses, or any other kinds of sewing, will be done at the above place."
Munro, ——	Savannah, Chatham Co.	1818	Intent to open day school; "plain Needle-Work."
Nye, Susan Davis	Augusta, Richmond Co.	1823–24	Born in New York; attended Litchfield Female Academy, CT; former preceptress of the female department of Raleigh Academy, NC; day school; "needle-work when desired." See Hutchison, Susan Davis (Nye).

Name	Location	Advertising Date(s)	Comments
Phillips' Academy	Savannah, Chatham Co.	1824–29	From Rockville Academy, SC; day and boarding school; Mrs. Phillips taught "needle work, marking, &c" in 1826; Miss Phillips taught "Needle Work, Marking and Flower Work" 1827–29.
Potter, ——	Savannah, Chatham Co.	1811	Miss Potter's School at Mrs. Battey's; "Embroidery, Needle-work on Muslin."
Raymond, Sarah			See Eudisco Academy; Female Academy, Warrenton.
Rhea, ——			See Sparta Academy.
Roma, ——	Savannah, Chatham Co.	1797	Day school; "Needle work of all kinds."
Rountree, ——	Petersburg, Wilkes Co.	1800	Intent to open school; taught in New York and then Augusta, Richmond Co.; "useful and ornamental art of Tambor, Embroidery, Lace-work, Plain Work."
Russell, —— and ——	Augusta, Richmond, Co.	1805	Intent to open day and boarding school; "Needle work in all its branches."
Sandwich, Leah (d. 1801)	Near Augusta, Richmond Co.	1795–1801	From England; first wife of Thomas Sandwich; operated a boarding school with husband and with assistance from daughter Diana Sophia Sandwich Lubbock; "useful and ornamental needleworks."
Sandwich, Margaret	Mount Salubrity (near Augusta), Richmond Co.	1802–1815	Second wife of Thomas Sandwich; "useful and ornamental Needle works."

Name	Location	Advertising Date(s)	Comments
——	Augusta, Richmond Co.	1817–1820	As a widow, operated a school with assistance from a Mrs. Hulbard; "Useful and ornamental needle work."
Shelton, Sarah B.	Savannah, Chatham Co.	1832	Intent to open day school; "Embroidery and Beadwork."
Simpson, ——	Savannah, Chatham Co.	1790	Intent to open a day and boarding school; "all Kinds of open and plain Needlework."
Sluyter, ——	Augusta, Richmond Co.	1804–5	Day and boarding school; "Needle Work."
Smith, Antoinetta	Savannah, Chatham Co.	1811–13	Born in Switzerland; taught in New Jersey; private school; "the different kinds of Needle-work, Embroidery, &c."
——	Near Bath and Augusta, Richmond Co.	1814	Instructor at Mount Enon Young Ladies School; "the various kinds of Needle-work, Netting, &c. such as Plain, Tambour and Embroidery."
——	Augusta, Richmond Co.	1815	Seminary; "plain and ornamental needle-work will be taught each day after the exercises of the school are over."
——	Augusta, Richmond Co.	1815	Consolidated her seminary with Richmond Academy; "all the branches of Needle-Work and other domestic acquirements."
Southern Female Seminary	St. Marys, Camden, Co.	1835	Under the direction of married couple —— and —— Robinson; "Embroidery."

Name	Location	Advertising Date(s)	Comments
Sparta Academy	Sparta, Hancock Co.	1823–24	Trustee-administered coeducational institution under the superintendence of Andrew Rhea; daughter —— Rhea in charge of female department; "Needle work."
Stebbens, Harriet	Mount Zion, Hancock Co.	1818	See Mount Zion Academy.
Stilwell, —— and ——	Savannah, Chatham Co.	1818	Intent to open school at residence; "Sewing and Embroidery."
Stone Mountain Academy	Stone Mountain, DeKalb Co.	1847	Trustee-administered, coeducational boarding institution; —— Dothart taught "Ornamental Needlework" for $4.00 per quarter.
Talifferro, ——	Washington, Wilkes Co.	1810	Day school; "plain needle-work."
Usher, ——	Monticello, Jasper Co.	1823–26	See Monticello Female Academy.
Veall, Elizabeth	Savannah, Chatham Co.	1781	Day school; "Sewing."
Washington Female Academy	Washington, Wilkes Co.	1814	Day and boarding school opened by ——Bowen under the inspection of the commissioners of the all-male Washington Academy; "Needle work of every kind taught, plain flowering and fancy work, embroidery and fillagree."
		1818	Female department under the direction of —— Douglass, from the North; "Needlework."
Wells, ——	Sunbury, Liberty Co.	1789–90	Half-day scholars; "several sorts of Needlework."

INDEX

References to illustrations are printed in bold type. The appendices are excluded from this index.